MUSIC SALES/LITTLE BLACK SONGBO
0-8256-3575-6   SONGBOOKS:ANTH/COLL 3   9/15/08
MAGERS‡QUINN BOOKSELLERS 180235

The
LITTLE BLACK
SONGBOOK

American
Favorites

A part of **The Music Sales Group**
New York/London/Paris/Sydney/Copenhagen/Berlin/Tokyo/Madrid

Copyright © 2008 Amsco Publications
A Division of Music Sales Corporation, New York

All rights reserved. No part of this book may be reproduced in any form
or by any electronic or mechanical means, including information storage
or retrieval systems, without permission in writing from the publisher,
except by a reviewer who may quote brief passages.

Order No. AM989483
ISBN-10: 0-8256-3575-6
ISBN-13: 978-0-8256-3575-5

Arrangements by Martin Shellard
Layout: Sol y Luna Creations

Exclusive Distributors:
Music Sales Corporation
257 Park Avenue South, New York, NY, 10010 USA
Music Sales Limited
14/15 Berners Street, London W1T 3LJ, England
Music Sales Pty. Limited
120 Rothschild Street, Rosebery, Sydney, NSW 2018, Australia

Printed in China

www.musicsales.com

The Air Force Hymn

Words by Mary C.D. Hamilton
Music by Henry Baker

Intro | D | D/F♯ |
            | G   A | D |

Verse 1

D   D/F♯   G   A   D
Lord guard and guide the men who fly,
D/F♯   Em A   D G   A
Through the great spa - ces of the sky,
                E7/G♯ E7   A
Be with them traversing the air,
D Dmaj7 D7 A   E7 Asus4 A7   D
In darken - ing storms or   sun   -   shine fair.

Verse 2

D   D/F♯   G   A   D
You who supported with tender might,
D/F♯   Em A   D G   A
The balanced birds in all their flight.
                E7/G♯   E7   A
Lord of the tempered winds be near,
D   Dmaj7 D7 A   E7 Asus4 A7 D
That, hav - ing you,   they know   no fear.

Link | D | D/F♯ |
           | G   A | D |

Copyright © 2008 Amsco Publications, a Division of Music Sales Corporation.
All Rights Reserved. International Copyright Secured.

Verse 3

D   D/F♯ G   A   D
Control their minds with instinct fit,
D/F♯   Em   A   D   G A
Whene'er, adventuring, they__ quit,
              E7/G♯ E7   A
The firm securi - ty of land;
D   Dmaj7 D7 A   E7 Asus4 A7 D
Grant stead - fast eye   and skill - ful hand.

Verse 4

D   D/F♯ G   A D
Aloft in soli - tude of space,
D/F♯   Em A   D G A
Uphold them with your saving grace.
           E7/G♯ E7   A
O God, protect the men who fly,
D   Dmaj7 D7 A   E7 Asus4 A7 D
Through lone - ly ways   be - neath the sky.

Alexander's Ragtime Band

Words and Music by Irving Berlin

Refrain

           F
Come on and hear, come on and hear,
C7   **F**
Alexander's ragtime band.
        B♭
Come on and hear, come on and hear,
               F+
It's the best band in the land.

      F
They can play a bugle call,

Like you never heard before,

So natural that you want to go to war.
C/E   **G7**   **C**
That's just the bestest band what am.

Verse 1

    C7
Oh, honey lamb,
        F
Come on along, come on along,
     C7   **F**
Let me take you by the hand.
     B♭
Up to the man, up to the man,

Who's the leader of the band.
    C7 **F**   **C7 F**
And if you care to   hear,
    Cm7 F7   **B♭**   **F°7**
That "Swa - nee River" played in ragtime,
           F
Come on and hear, come on and hear,
    C7   **F**
Alexander's Ragtime Band.

Copyright © 2008 Amsco Publications, a Division of Music Sales Corporation.
All Rights Reserved. International Copyright Secured.

Refrain

F
Come on and hear, come on and hear,
C7   **F**
Alexander's ragtime band.
B♭
Come on and hear, come on and hear,
          F+
It's the best band in the land.

F
They can play a bugle call,

Like you never heard before,

So natural that you want to go to war.
C/E   **G7**   **C**
That's just the bestest band what am.

Verse 2

C7
Oh, honey lamb,
    F
Come on along, come on along,
    C7   **F**
Let me take you by the hand.
    B♭
Up to the man, up to the man,

Who's the leader of the band.
    C7   **F**   **C7 F**
And if you care to   hear,
    Cm7 F7   **B♭**   **F°7**
That "Swa - nee River" played in ragtime,
       F
Come on and hear, come on and hear,
    C7   **F**
Alexander's Ragtime Band.

Amazing Grace

Words by John Newton
Traditional

Intro | **G** | **G7** | **C** | **D7** |

Verse 1

      G   **G7**   **C**   **G**
Amazing grace, how sweet the sound,
           A   **D**   **D7**
That saved a wretch like me!
 G   **G7**   **C**   **G**
I once was lost, but now am found,
    Em   **D7** **G**
Was blind but now I see.

Verse 2

      G   **G7**   **C**   **G**
'Twas grace that taught my heart to fear,
         A   **D**   **D7**
And grace my fears relieved;
   G   **G7**   **C**   **G**
How precious did that grace appear
  Em **D7** **G**
The hour I first believed.

Verse 3

    G   **G7**   **C**   **G**
The Lord has promised good to me,
        A   **D**   **D7**
His word my hope secures;
  G   **G7**   **C**   **G**
He will my shield and portion be,
  Em **D7** **G**
As long as life endures.

Copyright © 2008 Amsco Publications, a Division of Music Sales Corporation.
All Rights Reserved. International Copyright Secured.

Link

G	G7	C	G
	A	D	D7
G	G7	C	G
	Em	G	D7

Verse 4

      G   **G7**   **C**   **G**
When we've been here ten thousand years,
         A   **D**   **D7**
Bright shining as the sun,
    G   **G7**   **C**   **G**
We've no less days to sing God's praise,
    Em **D7**   **G**
Than when we'd first begun.

Verse 1

    G   **G7**   **C**   **G**
Amazing grace, how sweet the sound,
         A   **D**   **D7**
That saved a wretch like me!
 G   **G7** **C**   **G**
I once was lost, but now am found,
    Em   **D7** **G**
Was blind but now I see.

America

Words by Samuel Francis Smith
Traditional

Verse 1

G Em Am D7
My country,   'tis of thee,
G   Em Am G/D B7   Em
Sweet land of   li   -   ber - ty,
Am G/D D G
Of   thee I   sing;

Land where my fathers died,
D
Land of the pilgrims' pride,
G   C D G   D7/A   G/B
From ev'ry moun   -   tainside,
C   G/D D7 G
Let free - dom ring.

Verse 2

G Em Am D7
My na - tive country, thee,
G   Em Am G/D B7   Em
Land of   the   no   -   ble free,
Am G/D D G
Thy name I love.

I love thy rocks and rills,
D
Thy woods and templed hills;
G C   D   G D7/A   G/B
My heart with rap   -   ture thrills,
C   G/D D7 G
Like that a - bove.

Copyright © 2008 Amsco Publications, a Division of Music Sales Corporation.
All Rights Reserved. International Copyright Secured.

Verse 3

G Em Am D7
Let mu - sic   swell the breeze,
G   Em Am G/D B7   Em
And ring from all_____ the trees
Am   G/D D   G
Sweet free - dom's song;

Let mortal tongues awake,
D
Let all that breathe partake;
G   C   D   G D7/A   G/B
Let rocks their si   -   lence break,
C   G/D D7 G
The sound prolong.

Verse 4

G   Em Am   D7
Our fa - thers' God, to thee,
G Em Am G/D B7   Em
Author of   li - berty,
Am G/D D G
To thee we sing.

Long may our land be bright,
D
With freedom's holy light;
G C   D G D7/A   G/B
Protect us by_____ thy might,
C   G/D D7 G
Great God, our King.

13

America, The Beautiful

Words by Katherine Lee Bates
Music by Samuel A. Ward

Verse 1

    C   **G**
O beautiful for spacious skies,
    G7   **C**   **G7**
For amber waves of grain,___
   C   **G**
For purple mountain majesties,
 G°   **G** **D7**   **G**   **D7 G7**
Above   the fruited plain._____
 C   **G7**
America! America!
Dm7 G7   **F**   **G7 C**
God   shed his grace on thee,
F C **F**   **C**
   And crown thy good with brotherhood,
     F   **C** **G7 C**
From sea to shining sea.

Verse 2

    C   **G**
O beautiful for pilgrim feet,
     G7   **C**   **G7**
Whose stern impassioned stress,__
   C   **G**
A thoroughfare of freedom beat,
 G°   **G** **D7**   **G**   **D7 G7**
Across the wilderness._____
 C   **G7**
America! America!
Dm7 G7   **F** **G7 C**
God   mend thine ev'ry flaw,
F C **F**   **C**
   Confirm thy soul in self-control,
     F   **C G7 C**
Thy liberty in law.

Copyright © 2008 Amsco Publications, a Division of Music Sales Corporation.
All Rights Reserved. International Copyright Secured.

    C   **G**
O beautiful for heroes prov'd,
  G7   **C**   **G7**
In liberating strife.___
     C   **G**
Who more than self their country loved,
    G°   **G D7**   **G D7 G7**
And mer - cy more than life.
    C   **G**
America! America!
Dm7 G7   **F**   **G7 C**
May God thy gold re - fine,
F C   **F**   **C**
    Till all success be nobleness,
     F   **C**   **G7 C**
And ev'ry gain di - vine.

    C   **G**
O beautiful for patriot dream,
    G7   **C**   **G7**
That sees beyond the years,___
     C   **G**
Thine alabaster cities gleam,
   G°   **G D7**   **G**   **D7 G7**
Undimmed by human tears._____
   C   **G**
America! America!
Dm7 G7   **F**   **G7 C**
God   shed his grace on thee,
F C   **F**   **C**
    And crown thy good with brotherhood,
     F   **C**   **G7 C**
From sea to shining sea.

The American Flag

Words by Joseph Rodman Drake
Music by John W. Tufts

Verse 1

     G **Dsus4 D7 G**
When Freedom from her moun - tain height,
Dm6/F E **Am Am7/G D/F♯ Gsus4 G**
Un - furled her stan - dard to the air,_____
  D/F♯ **A7/E D♯°7**
She tore the azure robe of night,
   Em **C** **Am6 B**
And set the stars of glory there,
B/D♯ Em C G/B **C D7** **G**
And set the stars of glory there.___

Verse 2

     G   **Gsus4 D7 G**
Flag of the free heart's hope and home,
Dm6/F E **Am Am7/G D/F♯ Gsus4 G**
By angel hands to valor giv'n;____
  D/F♯ **A7/E D♯°7**
Thy stars have lit the welkin dome,
   Em **C**   **C** **Am B**
And all thy hues were born in heav'n,
B/D♯ Em C   **C** **Am B**
And all thy hues were born in heav'n.

Verse 3

     G **Dsus5 D7 G**
Forever float that stan - dard sheet,
Dm6/F E   **Am Am7/G D/F♯ Gsus4 G**
Where breathes the foe but falls be - fore us,
  D/F♯ **A7/E D♯°7**
With freedom's soil beneath our feet,
   Em   **C** **Am6** **B**
And freedom's banner streaming o'er us,
B/D♯ Em **C G/B C** **D7 G**
And freedom's banner streaming o'er us.

Copyright © 2008 Amsco Publications, a Division of Music Sales Corporation.
All Rights Reserved. International Copyright Secured.

Angels From The Realms Of Glory

Words by James Montgomery
Music by Henry Smar

Verse 1

A   **E7**   **A**
Angels from the realms   of glory,
D   **A**   **E**   **A**
Wing your flight o'er all the earth;
                   E7   **F♯m**   **C♯**
Ye who sang creation's sto   ry,
F♯m C♯ F♯m   **E B7 E**
Now proclaim Messi - ah's birth.

Refrain

             E7
Come and worship,
A   **A7**   **D**
Come   and worship,
Bm A   **A7**
Worship Christ,
Bm Bm7 E   **A**
The new - born King.

Verse 2

A   **E7**   **A**
Shepherds, in the field   abiding,
D   **A**   **E**   **A**
Watching o'er your flocks by night,
              E7 F♯m   **C♯**
God with us is now re - sid - ing;
F♯m C♯ F♯m   **E B7 E**
Yon - der shines the in - fant light.

Refrain

             E7
Come and worship,
A   **A7**   **D**
Come   and worship,
Bm A   **A7**
Worship Christ,
Bm Bm7 E   **A**
The new - born King.

Copyright © 2008 Amsco Publications, a Division of Music Sales Corporation.
All Rights Reserved. International Copyright Secured.

Verse 3

A   **E7**   **A**
Sages, leave your contemplations,
D   **A**   **E**   **A**
Brighter visions beam afar;
                E7 F♯m C♯
Seek the great desire of   nations;
F♯ C♯ F♯   **E B7 E**
Ye have seen His natal star.

Refrain

            E7
Come and worship,
A   **A7**   **D**
Come   and worship,
Bm A   A7
Worship Christ,
Bm Bm7 E   A
The new - born King.

Verse 4

A   **E7** **A**
Saints, before the altar bending,
D   **A**   **E**   **A**
Watching long in hope and fear;
             E7   **F♯m C♯**
Suddenly the Lord, de - scending,
F♯ C♯ F♯   **E**   **B7 E**
In   His temple shall ap - pear.

Refrain

            E7
Come and worship,
A   **A7**   **D**
Come   and worship,
Bm A   A7
Worship Christ,
Bm Bm7 E   A
The new - born King.

Verse 5

A   **E7**   **A**
Sinners, wrung with true repentance,
D   **A E**   **A**
Doomed for guilt to endless pains,
          E7   **F♯m C♯**
Justice now revokes the   sentence,
F♯ C♯ F♯   **E**   **B7 E**
Mercy   calls you; break your chains.

Refrain

                E7
Come and worship,
A   **A7**   **D**
Come   and worship,
Bm A   **A7**
Worship Christ,
Bm Bm7 E   **A**
The new - born King.

Verse 6

A   **E7**   **A**
All creation, join in praising God,
D   **A E**   **A**
The Father, Spirit, Son,
              E7   **F♯m C♯**
Evermore your voi - ces   raising,
F♯ C♯ F♯   **E**   **B7 E**
To th' eternal Three in   One.

Refrain

Come and worship,
A   **A7**   **D**
Come   and worship,
Bm A   **A7**
Worship Christ,
Bm Bm7 E   **A**
The new - born King.

Anchors Aweigh

Words by Alfred Hart Miles and R. Lovell
Music by Charles A. Zimmerman

Verse 1

C   Am
Stand Navy out to sea,
C   G7   C
Fight our battle cry.
F   C/E   E♭°7 G7/D
We'll never change our   course,
C D7   G7
So vicious foe steer shy.
C   Am
Roll out the T.N.T.,
C G7   C
Anchors aweigh.
F   C/E E♭°7 G7/D
Sail on to vic - to - ry,
C   C/G   G   C   G7
And sink their bones to Davy Jones, Hooray!

Verse 2

C   Am
Anchors aweigh, my boys,
C G7   C
Anchors aweigh.
F   C/E E♭°7 G7/D
Farewell to for - eign shores,
C D7   G
We sail at break of day.
C   Am
Through our last night on shore,
C   G7   C
Drink to the foam,
F   C/E E♭°7 G7/D
Until we meet once   more.
C   C/G   G   C   G7
Here's wishing you a happy voyage home.

Copyright © 2008 Amsco Publications, a Division of Music Sales Corporation.
All Rights Reserved. International Copyright Secured.

Verse 3

C   **Am**
Stand Navy, down the field,
C **G7** **C**
Sail to the sky.
F   **C/E**   **E♭°7 G7/D**
We'll never change our   course,
C **D7**   **G7**
So, Army you steer shy.
C   **Am**
Roll up the score, Navy,
C G7   **C**
Anchors aweigh.
F   **C/E**   **E♭°7 G7/D**
Sail, Navy, down the   field,
C   **C/G**   **G**   **C**
And sink the Army, sink the Army gray.

Angels We Have Heard On High

Traditional

Verse 1

F   **Gm7 C7 F**
Angels we have on heard on   high,
Dm   Am   B♭ F   G7   C7 F
Sweetly   singing on   the plain,
Dm   Am Dm F   Gm7 C   F
And the mountains in   reply,
Am   Gm   Dm Am F   C   F
Ech - o -   ing their joyous strain.

Refrain

Dm Gm7 C F B♭ C   F   C F Gm C7
"Glo   -   ry to God   in the   highest,
Dm Gm7 C F B♭ C   F   C F Gm C
Glo   -   ry to God   in the   highest."

Verse 2

F   **Gm7 C7   F**
Shepherds, why this ju - bi - lee?
Dm   Am   B♭ F   G7   C7 F
Why your joyful strains prolong?
Dm   Am Dm   F   Gm7 C   F
What the glad - some ti -   dings be,
Am   Gm   Dm Am F   C F
Which in - spire your heav'nly   song?

Refrain

Dm Gm7 C F B♭ C   F   C F Gm C7
"Glo   -   ry to God   in the   highest,
Dm Gm7 C F B♭ C   F   C F Gm C
Glo   -   ry to God   in the   highest."

Copyright © 2008 Amsco Publications, a Division of Music Sales Corporation.
All Rights Reserved. International Copyright Secured.

Verse 3

F   Gm7 C7 F
Come to Bethlehem   and see,
Dm   Am   B♭   F   G7 C7   F
Him whose birth the an - gels sing;
Dm   Am Dm F   Gm7   C   F
Come a - dore on bend - ed knee,
Am   Gm Dm   Am F   C   F
Christ, the Lord, the   newborn King.

Refrain

Dm Gm7 C F B♭ C   F   C F   Gm C7
"Glo   -   ry to God   in the   highest,
Dm Gm7 C F B♭ C   F   C F   Gm C
Glo   -   ry to God   in the   highest."

Verse 4

F   Gm7 C7 F
See Him in a man - ger   laid,
Dm   Am B♭   F G7 C7 F
Whom the   choirs of an - gels praise;
Dm Am Dm F   Gm7 C   F
Ma - ry, Jo - seph, lend   your aid,
Am   Gm Dm   Am F   C F
While our hearts in   love we raise.

Refrain

Dm Gm7 C F B♭ C   F   C F   Gm C7
"Glo   -   ry to God   in the   highest,
Dm Gm7 C F B♭ C   F   C F   Gm C
Glo   -   ry to God   in the   highest."

The Army Hymn

Words by Oliver Wendell Holmes
Music by Henry Baker

Verse 1

F   F/A   Bb6 C F
Oh, Lord of Hosts, Almighty King,
F/A   Gm C F Bb6 C
Behold the sa - crifice we bring,
    G7/B G7   C
To every arm thy strength impart;
F Fmaj7 F7 Bbmaj7 G7/B Csus4 C F
Thy spi - rit shed   through ev - ery heart.

Verse 2

F   F/A   Bb6 C F
Wake in our breasts the li - ving fires,
  F/A Gm C F   Bb6 C
The holy faith that warmed our sires;
    G7/B   G7   C
Thy hand hath made our nation free!
F Fmaj7 F7 Bbmaj7 G7/B Csus4 C F
To die for her is serv - ing Thee.

Verse 3

F   F/A Bb6 C F
Be Thou a pillar for to show,
  F/A   Gm C F Bb6 C
The midnight snare, the si - lent foe;
      G7/B G7   C
And when the battle thunders loud,
F Fmaj7 F7 Bbmaj7 G7/B Csus4 C F
Still guide us in   its mov - ing cloud.

Verse 4

F   F/A   Bb6 C F
God of all nations; Sovereign Lord,
F/A   Gm C F   Bb6 C
In Thy dread name we draw the sword,
  G7/B G7   C
We lift the starry flag on high,
F Fmaj7 F7 Bbmaj7 G7/B Csus4 C F
That fills with light our stor - my sky.

Copyright © 2008 Amsco Publications, a Division of Music Sales Corporation.
All Rights Reserved. International Copyright Secured.

Verse 5

F   F/A B♭6 C F
From treason's rent, from mur - der's stain,
F/A   Gm C F B♭6 C
Guard Thou its folds till peace shall reign,
     G7/B G7   C
Till fort and field, till shore and sea,
F Fmaj7 F7 B♭maj7 G7/B Csus4 C F
Join our loud an - them: Praise to thee!

A-Tisket A-Tasket

Traditional

Refrain 1

G7 C
A - tisket, a-tasket,
G7 C
A   green and yellow basket,
  G7
I brought a basket for my love,
                                            C
And on the way I dropped it.
G7 C
I   dropped it, I dropped it,
G7   C
Yes, on the way I dropped it,
  G7
A little girlie picked it up,
                              C
And took it to her love.

Verse

              F   **Fm**
She was truckin' on down the avenue,
        C   **G7**
Without a single thing to do,
              F   **Fm**
She was peck-peck-peckin' all around,
C   **G7**
When she spied it on the ground.

Refrain 2

        C
A tisket, a-tasket,
G7 C
She took my yellow basket,
        G7
And if she doesn't bring it back,
                        C
I think that I shall die.

Copyright © 2008 Amsco Publications, a Division of Music Sales Corporation.
All Rights Reserved. International Copyright Secured.

Away Rio

Traditional

Verse 1

      E   B7   E
The anchor is weighed and sails they are set.

Away, Rio.
  A   E   B7   E
The maids we are leaving we'll never forget,
                       B7 E
And we're bound for the Rio Grande.

Refrain

            B7 E
And away,__ Rio, away, Rio,
    A   E   B7   E
We're bound away on this very day,
                B7 E
Yes, we're bound for the Rio Grande.

Verse 2

      E   B7   E
So it's pack up your donkey and get underway,

Away, Rio.
  A   E   B7   E
The girls we are leaving can take half our pay,
                   B7 E
And we're bound for the Rio Grande.

Refrain

            B7 E
And away,__ Rio, away, Rio,
    A   E   B7   E
We're bound away on this very day,
                B7 E
Yes, we're bound for the Rio Grande.

Copyright © 2008 Amsco Publications, a Division of Music Sales Corporation.
All Rights Reserved. International Copyright Secured.

Verse 3

            E   **B7**   **E**
We've a jolly good ship and a jolly good crew,

Away, Rio.
  A   **E**   **B7**   **E**
A jolly good mate and a good skipper too,
                B7 E
And we're bound for the Rio Grande.

Refrain

        B7 E
And away,__ Rio, away, Rio,
    A   **E**   **B7**   **E**
We're bound away on this very day,
          B7 E
Yes, we're bound for the Rio Grande.

Verse 4

E   **B7**   **E**
Goodbye to Sally and goodbye to Sue,

Away Rio.
  A   **B7**   **E**
And you who are listening, goodbye to you too,
           B7 E
And we're bound for the Rio Grande.

Refrain

        B7 E
And away,__ Rio, away, Rio,
    A   **E**   **B7**   **E**
We're bound away on this very day,
          B7 E
Yes, we're bound for the Rio Grande.

Verse 5

    E   **B7**   **E**
Heave with a will, heave long and strong,

Away Rio.
A   **B7**   **E**
Sing the good chorus, for 'tis a good song,
                                B7 E
Yes, we're bound for the Rio Grande.

Refrain

             B7 E
And away,__ Rio, away, Rio,
        A   **E**   **B7**   **E**
We're bound away on this very day,
                           B7 E
Yes, we're bound for the Rio Grande.

Verse 6

        E   **B7**   **E**
The chains up and down, the bosun did say,

Away Rio.
A   **B7**   **E**
Heave up the hause pipe, the anchor's away,
                        B7 E
Yes, we're bound for the Rio Grande.

Refrain

             B7 E
And away,__ Rio, away, Rio,
        A   **E**   **B7**   **E**
We're bound away on this very day,
                         B7 E
Yes, we're bound for the Rio Grande.

The Band Played On

Words by John F. Palmer
Music by John F. Palmer and Charles B. Ward

Refrain

G   **Bm/F♯**
Casey would waltz,
          Em7   **G/D**
With the strawberry blond,
    D7
And the band played on.

He'd glide 'cross the floor,

With the girl he adored,
      G   **Bm/F♯**
And the band played on.
Em7   **G**   **D7**
    But his brain was so loaded,
  G7   **C/G**
It nearly exploded,
    C   **Am**
The poor girl would shake with alarm,
      C   **C♯°7**
He'd ne'er leave the girl,
      G/D
With the strawberry curl,
    A7 **D7**   **G**
And the band played on.

Copyright © 2008 Amsco Publications, a Division of Music Sales Corporation.
All Rights Reserved. International Copyright Secured.

Battle Hymn Of The Republic

Words by Julia Ward Howe
Traditional

Verse 1

     G
Mine eyes have seen the glory of the coming of the Lord;
  C   **G**
He is trampling out the vintage where the grapes of wrath are stored;

He has loosed the fateful lightning of His terrible swift sword;
  Am   **G**   **D** **G**
His truth is marching on.

Refrain

Glory! Glory! Hallelujah!
C   **G**
Glory! Glory! Hallelujah!
                 Em
Glory! Glory! Hallelujah!
Am   **G**   **D** **G**
His truth is marching on.

Verse 2

I have seen Him in the watchfires of a hundred circling camps,
       C   **G**
They have builded Him an altar in the evening dews and damps,

I can read His righteous sentence by the dim and flaring lamps,
Am G   **D G**
His day is marching on.

Refrain

Glory! Glory! Hallelujah!
C   **G**
Glory! Glory! Hallelujah!
                 Em
Glory! Glory! Hallelujah!
Am   **G**   **D** **G**
His truth is marching on.

Copyright © 2008 Amsco Publications, a Division of Music Sales Corporation.
All Rights Reserved. International Copyright Secured.

Verse 3   I have read a fiery Gospel writ in burnished rows of steel:
            C   **G**
"As ye deal with My contemners, so with you My grace shall deal."

Let the Hero, born of woman, crush the serpent with His heel,
      Am   **G**   **D G**
Since God is marching on.

Refrain   Glory! Glory! Hallelujah!
    C   **G**
Glory! Glory! Hallelujah!
                        Em
Glory! Glory! Hallelujah!
    Am   **G**   **D G**
His truth is marching on.

Verse 4   He has sounded forth the trumpet that shall never call retreat,
      C   **G**
He is sifting out the hearts of men before His judgment seat.

Oh, be swift, my soul, to answer Him, be jubilant, my feet!
    Am   **G**   **D G**
Our God is marching on.

Refrain   Glory! Glory! Hallelujah!
    C   **G**
Glory! Glory! Hallelujah!
                        Em
Glory! Glory! Hallelujah!
    Am   **G**   **D G**
His truth is marching on.

Verse 5   In the beauty of the lilies Christ was born across the sea,
                     C   **G**
            With a glory in His bosom that transfigures you and me.

            As He died to make men holy, let us live to make men free,
                     Am   **G**   **D G**
            While God is marching on.

Refrain   Glory! Glory! Hallelujah!
            C   **G**
            Glory! Glory! Hallelujah!
                            Em
            Glory! Glory! Hallelujah!
               Am   **G**   **D G**
            His truth is marching on.

Verse 6   He is coming like the glory of the morning on the wave,
                     C   **G**
            He is wisdom to the mighty, He is honor to the brave.

            So the world shall be His footstool, and the soul of wrong His slave,
               Am   **G**   **D G**
            Our God is marching on.

Refrain   Glory! Glory! Hallelujah!
            C   **G**
            Glory! Glory! Hallelujah!
                            Em
            Glory! Glory! Hallelujah!
               Am   **G**   **D G**
            His truth is marching on.

The Banks Of The Ohio

Traditional

Intro | **D** | **A7** | **D** |

Verse 1

        D   **A7**
I asked my love to take a walk,
                   D
To take a walk, just a little walk.
D7   **G**
Down beside, where the waters flow,
         D   **A7**   **D**
Down by the banks   of the Ohio.

Verse 2

        D   **A7**
And only say that you'll be mine,
            D
In no other arms entwine.
D7   **G**
Down beside, where the waters flow,
        D   **A7**   **D**
Down by the banks   of the Ohio.

Link | **D** | | **A7** | | |
          | | | **D** | | |

Copyright © 2008 Amsco Publications, a Division of Music Sales Corporation.
All Rights Reserved. International Copyright Secured.

Verse 3

          D   A7
I held a knife against her breast.
                   D
As into my arms she pressed.
          D7   G
She cried "Oh Willie, don't you murder me;
        D   A7   D
I'm not prepared   for eternity."

Verse 4

          D   A7
I started home 'tween twelve and one.
                      D
I cried, "My God, what have I done?"
        D7   G
Killed the only woman I loved.
        D   A7   D
Because she would   not be my bride.

Blow The Man Down

Traditional

Verse 1

       F
Come all ye young fellows that follow the sea,
     D7 Gm   **C7**
To me way, hey, blow the man down,

And pray, pay attention and listen to me,
            F
Give me some time to blow the man down.

Verse 2

       F
As I was walkin' down Paradise Street,
     D7 Gm   **C7**
To me way, hey, blow the man down,

A pretty young damsel I chanced for to meet,
            F
Give me some time to blow the man down.

Verse 3

       F
And as we were going she said unto me,
     D7 Gm   **C7**
To me way, hey, blow the man down,

There's a spanking full-rigger just ready for sea,
            F
Give me some time to blow the man down.

Verse 4

       F
As soon as that packet was out on the sea,
     D7 Gm   **C7**
To me way, hey, blow the man down,

'Twas devilish hard treatment of every degree,
            F
Give me some time to blow the man down.

Copyright © 2008 Amsco Publications, a Division of Music Sales Corporation.
All Rights Reserved. International Copyright Secured.

Verse 5

         F
So I give you fair warning before we belay,
   D7 Gm   **C7**
To me way, hey, blow the man down,

Don't ever take heed of what pretty girls say,
                 F
Give me some time to blow the man down.

Bridal Chorus

Richard Wagner

Verse 1

G
Guided by us,
   D7 **G**
Thrice happy pair,
     C/G **G**
Enter the door - way,
   A7   **D7**
'Tis love invites,
G   **D7**   **G**
All that is brave, all that is fair,
           Em   **Am D7** **G**
Love now triumphant, forev - er unites,
Am G Am C   **D G   D**
Champion of   virtue boldly advance,
Am G Am C   **E   B   E**
Flower of   beauty, gently advance.
      A E   A6 E B B7 B♭   **B**
Now the loud mirth of rev'ling is ended,
E   **F♯7**   **B**
Night bringing peace and bliss has descended;
E   **Em** **G/B**   **D7**   **G**
Fanned by the breath of happiness, rest,
               D7   **Bm F♯** **B**
Closed to the world, by love only blest!
D7   **G**
   Guided by us,
     D7   **G**
Thrice happy pair,
     C/G G
Enter the doorway,
   A7   **D7**
'Tis love invites,
G   **D7**   **G**
All that is brave, all that is fair,
           Em   **Am7 D7**   **G**
Love now triumphant, forev - er unites.

Copyright © 2008 Amsco Publications, a Division of Music Sales Corporation.
All Rights Reserved. International Copyright Secured.

G

Verse 2   Home joys divine,
   D7   G
   Home joys so pure,
        C/G   G
   Love ever faith - ful,
      A7   D7
   And love ever sure.
   G   **D7   G**
   All that is brave, all that is fair,
                Em   **Am D7 G**
   Love now triumphant, forev - er unites,
   Am G Am C   D   G   D
   Champion of   virtue boldly advance,
   Am G Am C   E   B   E
   Flower of   beauty, gently advance.
          A   E   A6   E B   B7 B♭   B
   Now the loud mirth of rev'ling is ended,
   E   **F♯7   B**
   Night bringing peace and bliss has descended;
   E   Em   G/B   D7   G
   Fanned by the breath of happiness, rest,
                D7   Bm F♯   B
   Closed to the world, by love only blest!
   D7   G
      Home joys divine,
         D7   G
   Home joys so pure,
         C/G   G
   Love ever faith - ful,
      A7   D7
   And love ever sure;
   G   **D7   G**
   All that is brave, all that is fair,
                Em   **Am7 D7   G**
   Love now triumphant, forev -   er unites.

39

Bury Me Not
On The Lone Prairie

Traditional

Verse 1

    D
    "Oh, bury me not on the lone prairie,
           Em   **D**
    These words came slow and mournfully.

    From the pallid lips of the youth who lay,
           Em   **A7**   **D**
    On his dying bed   at the close of day.

Verse 2

    "Oh, bury me not on the lone prairie
              Em7   **D**
    Where the wild coyotes will howl o'er me.

    In a narrow grave, just six by three,
           Em7 **A7**   **D**
    Oh, bury me not   on the lone prairie."

Verse 3

    "It matters not, I've oft been told,
           Em7   **D**
    Where the body lies when the heart grows cold.

    Yet grant, oh grant this wish to me,
           Em7 **A7**   **D**
    Oh, bury me not   on the lone prairie."

Verse 4

    "I've always wished to be laid when I die,
             Em7   **D**
    In the little churchyard on the green hillside.

    By my father's grave, there let mine be,
           Em7 **A7**   **D**
    Oh, bury me not   on the lone prairie."

Copyright © 2008 Amsco Publications, a Division of Music Sales Corporation.
All Rights Reserved. International Copyright Secured.

Verse 5 "Oh, bury me not," and his voice failed there,
Em7   **D**
But we took no heed to his dying prayer.

In a narrow grave, just six by three,
Em7 A7   **D**
We buried him there   on the lone prairie.

Verse 6 And the cowboys now as they cross the plains,
Em7
For they marked the spot,
D
Where his bones are lain.

Fling a handful of roses o'er his grave
Em7 A7   **D**
With a prayer to Him, who his soul will save.

The Caissons Go Rolling Along

Music and Words by Edmund L. Gruber

Intro | **G7** | | |

             | **C** | | |

C

Verse 1 Over hill, over dale,

As we hit the dusty trail,
C♯°7   **G7**   **C**
And the caissons go rolling along.

In and out, hear them shout:

"Counter march and right about."
C♯°7   **G7**   **C**
And the caissons go rolling along.

                   C

Refrain For it's hi! hi! hee!
              F   **C**
In the Field Artillery,
Am   **D7**   **G7**
Shoot out your numbers loud and strong,
              C **Am** **E7**
For where'er you go,
F   **C**
You will always know,
Am Fm G7   **C**
That the   caissons are rolling along.
C♯°7   **G7**   **C**
That those caissons are rolling along.

Copyright © 2008 Amsco Publications, a Division of Music Sales Corporation.
All Rights Reserved. International Copyright Secured.

Verse 2

C
In the storm, in the night,

Action left or action right,
C♯°7   **G7**   **C**
See those caissons go rolling along,

Limber front, limber rear,

Prepare to mount your cannoneer,
C♯°7   **G7**   **C**
And those caissons go rolling along.

Refrain

         C
For it's hi! hi! hee!
      F   **C**
In the Field Artillery,
Am   **D7**   **G7**
Shoot out your numbers loud and strong,
       C   **Am** **E7**
For where'er you   go,
F   **C**
You will always know,
Am **Fm** **G7**   **C**
That the   caissons are rolling along.
C♯°7   **G7**   **C**
That those caissons are rolling along.

The Camptown Races

Words and Music by Stephen Foster

Verse 1

D
The Camptown ladies sing this song,
A7
Doo-dah! Doo-dah!
D
The Camptown racetrack's five miles long,
A7
Oh, doo-dah day!

Refrain

D
Goin' to run all night,
G
Goin' to run all day,

I bet my money on a bob-tailed nag,
C   **A7**   **D**
Somebody bet on the bay.

Verse 2

D
I come down there with my hat caved in,
A7
Doo-dah! Doo-dah!
D
I go back home with a pocket full of tin,
A7
Oh! De doo-dah day!

Refrain

D
Goin' to run all night,
G
Goin' to run all day,

I bet my money on a bob-tailed nag,
C   **A7**   **D**
Somebody bet on the bay.

Copyright © 2008 Amsco Publications, a Division of Music Sales Corporation.
All Rights Reserved. International Copyright Secured.

Verse 3

   D
The long tail filly and the big black horse,
A7
Doo-dah! Doo-dah!
   D
They fly the track and they both cut across,
A7
Oh, de doo-dah day!
   D
The blind horse stickin' in a big mud hole,
A7
Doo-dah! Doo-dah!
D
Can't touch bottom with a ten foot pole,
A7
Oh! De doo-dah day!

Refrain

D
Goin' to run all night,
G
Goin' to run all day,

I bet my money on a bob-tailed nag,
C   **A7** **D**
Somebody bet on the bay.

Verse 4

D
Old muley cow comes on to the track,
A7
Doo-dah! Doo-dah!
  D
The bob-tail fling her over his back,
A7
Oh! De doo-dah day!
   D
Then fly along like a rail-road car,
A7
Doo-dah! Doo-dah!
D
Runnin' a race with a shootin' star,
A7
Oh! De doo-dah day!

Verse 5

D
See them flyin' on a ten mile heat,
A7
Doo-dah! Doo-dah!
D
Round the race track, then repeat,
A7
Oh! Doo-dah day!
  D
I win my money on the bob-tail nag,
A7
Doo-dah! Doo-dah!
  D
I keep my money in an old tow-bag,
A7
Oh! De doo-dah day!

Refrain

D
Goin' to run all night,
G
Goin' to run all day,

I bet my money on a bob-tailed nag,
C   **A7**   **D**
Somebody bet on the bay.

The Church's One Foundation

Words by Samuel J. Stone
Music by Samuel S. Wesley

Verse 1

F   B♭ F   B♭
The church's one foundation,
F Gm7 C7   F
Is Jesus Christ her Lord;
C7 F   F+ A7 B♭° B♭
She is his new cre - a - tion,
C B♭ C F G7 C
By wa - ter and the Word.
F   C7 F   B♭   F
From heav'n He came and sought her,
Dm A7   Dm D Gm
To be_____ his ho - ly bride;
C7   F   B♭   F B♭
    With His own blood he bought her,
F   Gm7 C7   F
And for her life he died.

Verse 2

F   B♭ F B♭
Elect from every nation,
F Gm7 C7   F
Yet one o'er all the earth;
C7 F   F+ A7 B♭° B♭
Her charter of   sal - va - tion,
C B♭ C F   G7 C
One Lord, one faith, one birth;
F   C7 F   B♭   F
One ho - ly name she blesses,
Dm A7   Dm D Gm
Partakes__ one ho - ly food,
C7   F   B♭ F B♭
    And to one hope she presses,
F   Gm7 C7   F
With every grace endued.

Copyright © 2008 Amsco Publications, a Division of Music Sales Corporation.
All Rights Reserved. International Copyright Secured.

      F   **B♭** **F B♭**
Though with a scornful wonder,
F **Gm7** **C7**   **F**
We see her sore oppressed,
C7 F   **F+ A7 B♭° B♭**
By schisms rent a - sun - der,
C **B♭** **C** **F** **G7** **C**
By he - re - sies dis - tressed,
     F   **C7 F**   **B♭**
Yet saints their watch are keeping;
F   **Dm A7 Dm** **D**   **Gm**
Their cry goes up, "How long?"
C7   **F**   **B♭** **F B♭**
   And soon the night of weeping,
F   **Gm7 C7**   **F**
Shall be the morn of song.

      F   **B♭** **F B♭**
'Mid toil and tri - bulation,
F   **Gm7 C7**   **F**
And tumult of her war,
C7 F   **F+ A7 B♭° B♭**
She waits the con - summa - tion,
C **B♭**   **C F G7** **C**
Of peace forever - more;
     F   **C7 F**   **B♭**
Till, with the vision glorious,
F **Dm A7 Dm** **D** **Gm**
Her long - ing eyes are blest,
C7   **F**   **B♭**   **F B♭**
   And the great church victorious,
F   **Gm7 C7**   **F**
Shall be the church at rest.

Verse 5

    F   **B♭** **F**   **B♭**
Yet she on earth hath union,
F   **Gm7**   **C7**   **F**
With God the Three in One,
C7 F   **F+**   **A7 B♭°**   **B♭**
And mystic sweet commun - ion,
C   **B♭** **C**   **F** **G7** **C**
With those whose rest is   won.
   F   **C7** **F** **B♭**
O happy ones and holy!
F   **Dm A7 Dm** **D** **Gm**
Lord, give us   grace that we,
C7 **F**   **B♭ F**   **B♭**
Like them, the meek and lowly,
F **Gm7**   **C7**   **F**
On high may dwell with thee.

Carry Me Back To Old Virginny

Words and Music by James A. Bland

Refrain

G   C G
Carry me back to old Virginny,
       C G A7   A°7 A7 D
There's where the cotton and the corn and 'ta - toes grow,
D7 G   C   G   G7 C C7 G
There's where the birds warble sweet in the springtime,
         C G G/D D7 G/D D7 G
There's where my old, weary heart___ longs to go,

Verse 1

D7   G
There's where I labored so hard for my loved ones,
    Em   A7   D7
Day after day in the field of yellow corn,
G C   G   C C♯°7 G
No place on earth do I love more sincerely,
        C G/D D7 G/D D7 G
Than old Virginny, the state where I was born.

Refrain

G   C G
Carry me back to old Virginny,
       C G A7   A°7 A7 D
There let me live till I wither and de - cay,
D7 G C G   G7   C   C7 G
Long by the old Dismal Swamp have I wandered,
         C G G/D D7 G/D D7 G
There's where this old dreamer's life will pass a - way.

Copyright © 2008 Amsco Publications, a Division of Music Sales Corporation.
All Rights Reserved. International Copyright Secured.

Verse 2

D7   G

Momma and poppa have long gone before me;

                Em   A7   D7

Soon we will meet on that bright and golden shore.

G   C   G   C C♯°7   G

There we'll be happy and free from all sorrow,

                         C   G/D D7 G/D D7 G

There's where we'll meet and we'll ne - ver part no more.

Refrain

G   C   G

Carry me back to old Virginny,

                      C G A7   A°7 A7 D

There's where the cotton and the corn and 'ta - toes grow,

D7 G   C   G   G7   C   C7   G

    There's where the birds warble sweet in the springtime,

                      C   G G/D D7 G/D   D7 G

There's where my old, weary heart____ longs to go.

Christ The Lord Is Risen Today

Words by Charles Wesley

Traditional

Verse 1

```
C                      F      F/C C   G7 C   G7 C
Christ, the Lord, is ris'n today,   Al - lelu - ia!
F/A C/G F      C/E G7sus4 G7 C/G G C  G7 C    G7 C
Sons of  men and an  -  gels say:___ Al - lelu - ia!
G           G7 C G    C   G D7 G C G/D D7 G
Raise your joys and triumphs high, Al - le - lu  -  ia!
      G7 C        F      F/C C   Dm C C/G G C
Sing, ye  heav'ns, and earth, reply,___ Al - le lu  - ia!
```

Verse 2

```
C               F    F/C C    G7 C   G7 C
Love's redeeming work is done,  Al - lelu - ia!
F/A  C/G F    C/E G7sus4 G7 C/G G C  G7 C   G7 C
Fought the fight, the bat  -  tle won,__ Al - lelu - ia!
G           G7 C    G C    G D7 G C G/D D7 G
Lo, the Sun's e - clipse is over, Al - le - lu  -  ia!
     G7 C    F      F/C C    Dm C C/G G C
Lo, He  sets in blood no more,  Al - le lu  -  ia!
```

Verse 3

```
C               F      F/C C   G7 C   G7 C
Vain the stone, the watch, the seal,  Al - lelu - ia!
F/A  C/G F    C/E G7sus4 G7 C/G G C  G7 C   G7 C
Christ hath burst the gates of  hell,____ Al - lelu - ia!
G           G7 C  G  C    G D7 G C G/D D7 G
Death in vain forbids His rise, Al - le - lu  -  ia!
     G7 C       F  F/C C    Dm C C/G G C
Christ hath opened paradise,   Al - le lu  -  ia!
```

Verse 4

```
C            F       F/C C   G7 C   G7 C
Lives again our glorious King,  Al - lelu - ia!
F/A  C/G F    C/E G7sus4 G7 C/G G C G7 C    G7 C
Where, O  death, is  now      thy sting?__ Al - lelu - ia!
G           G7 C    G C    G D7 G C G/D D7 G
Once He died our souls to save, Al - le - lu  -  ia!
     G7 C     F F/C C      Dm C C/G G C
Where thy victory, O  grave? Al - le lu  -  ia!
```

Copyright © 2008 Amsco Publications, a Division of Music Sales Corporation.
All Rights Reserved. International Copyright Secured.

Verse 5

C		F		F/C	C		G7	C		G7	C

Soar we now where Christ hath led,   Al - lelu - ia!

F/A C/G F C/E G7sus4 G7 C/G G C G7 C G7 C

Fol - low - ing our exal - ted Head,__ Al - lelu - ia!

G G7 C G C G D7 G C G/D D7 G

Made like Him, like Him we rise, Al - le - lu - ia!

G7 C F F/C C Dm C C/G G C

Ours the cross, the grave, the skies, Al - le lu - ia!

Verse 6

C F F/C C G7 C G7 C

Hail, the Lord of earth and Heav'n, Al - lelu - ia!

F/A C/G F C/E G7sus4 G7 C/G G C G7 C G7 C

Praise to Thee by both   be giv'n__, Al - lelu - ia!

G G7 C G C G D7 G C G/D D7 G

Thee we greet tri - umphant now, Al - le - lu - ia!

G7 C F F/C C Dm C C/G G C

Hail, the resurrection, thou, Al - le lu - ia!

Christ Was Born On Christmas Day

Traditional

Verse 1

```
F       Dm      C          F
Christ was born on Christmas Day,
           F/E   B♭/D    C
Wreathe the holly, twine the bay;
B♭           C7
Christus natus hodie;
     F          Dm     B♭  C7    F
The Babe, The Son, the Holy One of Mary.
```

Verse 2

```
F   Dm   C    F
He is born to set us free,
        F/E      B♭/D   C
He is born our Lord to be,
B♭        C7
Ex Maria Virgine,
     F        Dm      B♭ C7     F
The God, the Lord, by all ador'd forever.
```

Verse 3

```
F     Dm      C       F
Let the bright red berries glow,
      F/E      B♭/D   C
Ev'rywhere in goodly show,
B♭            C7
Christus natus hodie;
     F          Dm     B♭  C7    F
The Babe, The Son, the Holy One of Mary.
```

Verse 4

```
F       Dm   C        F
Christian men, rejoice and sing,
        F/E      B♭/D  C
'Tis the birthday of a    King
B♭        C7
Ex Maria Virgine;
     F        Dm      B♭ C7     F
The God, the Lord, by all ador'd forever.
```

Copyright © 2008 Amsco Publications, a Division of Music Sales Corporation.
All Rights Reserved. International Copyright Secured.

Clementine

Words and Music by Percy Montrose

Verse 1

        F
In a cavern, in a canyon,
        C7
Excavating for a mine,
           F
Dwelt a miner, forty-niner,
C7   **F**
And his daughter Clementine.

Chorus

Oh my darling, oh my darling,
        C7
Oh my darling Clementine.
           F
You are lost and gone forever,
C7   **F**
Dreadful sorry, Clementine.

Verse 2

      F
Light she was, and like a fairy,
           C7
And her shoes were number nine,
         F
Herring boxes without topses,
C7   **F**
Sandals were for Clementine.

Chorus

Oh my darling, oh my darling,
        C7
Oh my darling Clementine.
          F
You are lost and gone forever,
C7   **F**
Dreadful sorry, Clementine.

Copyright © 2008 Amsco Publications, a Division of Music Sales Corporation.
All Rights Reserved. International Copyright Secured.

Verse 3

           F
Drove she ducklings to the water
              C7
Ev'ry morning just at nine,
              F
Hit her foot against a splinter,
C7   **F**
Fell into the foaming brine.

Chorus

Oh my darling, oh my darling,
              C7
Oh my darling Clementine.
              F
You are lost and gone forever,
C7   **F**
Dreadful sorry, Clementine.

Verse 4

      F
Ruby lips above the water,
              C7
Blowing bubbles soft and fine,
              F
Alas for me! I was no swimmer,
C7   **F**
So I lost my Clementine.

Chorus

Oh my darling, oh my darling,
              C7
Oh my darling Clementine.
              F
You are lost and gone forever,
C7   **F**
Dreadful sorry, Clementine.

Colorado Trail

Traditional

Chorus

D
Weep all ye little rains,
G   D
Wail wind, wail,
   Bm F#m D7
All along, all   along,
   G   Gm D
The Colorado trail.

Verse 1

Eyes like the morning star,
G   D
Lips like a rose,

Jennie was a pretty gal,
E7   A7
God almighty knows!

Chorus

D
Weep all ye little rains,
G   D
Wail wind, wail,
   Bm F#m D7
All along, all   along,
   G   Gm D
The Colorado trail.

Verse 2

Ride all the lonely nights,
G   D
Ride through the day.

Keep the herd a movin' on,
E7   A7
Movin' on its way.

Copyright © 2008 Amsco Publications, a Division of Music Sales Corporation.
All Rights Reserved. International Copyright Secured.

Chorus
D
Weep all ye little rains,
G   **D**
Wail wind, wail,
    Bm F#m D7
All along, all   along,
    G   Gm D
The Colorado trail.

Verse 3
Ride through the stormy night,
G   **D**
Dark is the sky.

I wish I'd stayed in Abilene,
E7   **A7**
Nice and warm and dry.

Chorus
D
Weep all ye little rains,
G   **D**
Wail wind, wail,
    Bm F#m D7
All along, all   along,
    G   Gm D
The Colorado trail.

Columbia, The Gem
Of The Ocean

Words and Music by David T. Shaw and Thomas A. Becket

Verse 1

      A   **E**   **A**
Oh Columbia! the gem of the ocean,
     D   **D♯°7 A/E E**
The home of the brave and the   free,___
               B7   **E**
The shrine of each patriot's devotion,
  B7   **E**
A world offers homage to thee.
  E7   **A**
Thy mandates make heroes assemble,
               E
When Liberty's form stands in view;
 A   **D**
Thy banners make tyranny tremble
 E7   **A**
When borne by the red, white and blue!
 E   **A**
When borne by the red, white and blue!
 E   **A**
When borne by the red, white and blue!
            D
Thy banners make tyranny tremble,
 E7   **A**
When borne by the red, white and blue.

Copyright © 2008 Amsco Publications, a Division of Music Sales Corporation.
All Rights Reserved. International Copyright Secured.

Verse 2

        A   **E**   **A**
When war winged its wide desolation,
  D   **D♯°7 A/E E**
And threatened the land to de - form,__
          B7   **E**
The ark then of freedom's foundation,
  B7   **E**
Columbia, rode safe through the storm:
     E7   **A**
With the garlands of vict'ry around her,
                  E
When so proudly she bore her brave crew,
    A   **D**
With her flag proudly floating before her,
  E7   **A**
The boast of the red, white and blue,
  E   **A**
The boast of the red, white and blue,
  E   **A**
The boast of the red, white and blue,
           D
With her flag proudly floating before her,
  E7   **A**
The boast of the red, white and blue.

Verse 3

      A   E   A
The star-spangled banner bring hither,
     D   D♯°7 A/E E
O'er Columbia's true sons let it   wave;__
     B7   E
May the wreaths of the heroes ne'er wither,
     B7   E
Nor its stars cease to shine on the brave;
     E7   A
May the service, united, ne'er sever,
                       E
But hold to their colors so true;
     A   D
The Army and Navy forever!
     E7   A
Three cheers for the red, white and blue,
     E   A
Three cheers for the red, white and blue,
     E   A
Three cheers for the red, white and blue,
              D
The Army and Navy forever!
     E7   A
Three cheers for the red, white and blue.

Coventry Carol

Traditional

Verse 1

Gm   D   Gm Cm D
Lullay, Thou little tiny Child,
Gm D Gm C D7 Gm
Bye, bye, lul - ly, lul - lay.
B♭ F B♭   F B♭ Cm D
Lullay, Thou lit - tle tiny Child.
Gm D Gm Cm D G
Bye, bye, lul - ly, lul - lay.

Verse 2

Gm D Gm   Cm   D
O sisters, too, how may we do,
Gm D Gm C   D7 Gm
For to pre - serve this day;
B♭ F B♭   F B♭ Cm   D
This poor Youngling for whom we sing,
Gm D Gm Cm D G
Bye, bye, lul - ly, lul - lay.

Verse 3

Gm   D Gm Cm   D
Herod the King, in his raging,
Gm D Gm C   D7 Gm
Charged he   hath this day;
B♭ F   B♭   F   B♭ Cm D
His men of might, in his own sight,
Gm D Gm Cm   D G
All   children   young, to slay.

Verse 4

Gm   D   Gm   Cm   D
Then woe is me, poor Child, for Thee,
Gm D Gm C   D7 Gm
And ev - er mourn and say;
B♭ F B♭   F B♭ Cm D
For Thy parting, nor say nor sing,
Gm D Gm Cm D G
Bye, bye, lul - ly, lul - lay.

Copyright © 2008 Amsco Publications, a Division of Music Sales Corporation.
All Rights Reserved. International Copyright Secured.

Cradle Song

Words by Karl Simrock
Music by Johannes Brahms

Intro | **A7** | **D** |

Verse 1   Lullaby and goodnight,
                    A7
With roses delight,

Creep into thy bed,
               D
There pillow thy head.
    G   **D**
If God will thou shalt wake,
        A7   **D**
When the morning doth break,
    G   **D**
If God will thou shalt wake,
        A7   **D**
When the morning doth break.

Verse 2   Lullaby and goodnight,
                     A7
Those blue eyes close tight,

Bright angels are near,
               D
So sleep without fear,
    G   **D**
They will guard thee from harm,
        A7   **D**
With fair dreamland's sweet charm,
    G   **D**
They will guard thee from harm,
        A7   **D**
With fair dreamland's sweet charm.

Copyright © 2008 Amsco Publications, a Division of Music Sales Corporation.
All Rights Reserved. International Copyright Secured.

Dixie

Words and Music by Daniel Decatur Emmett

Verse 1

    C   G7   C
I wish I was in the land of cotton,
F
Old times there are not forgotten,
     C7
Look away, look away,
     G7   C
Look away, Dixieland!
     G7   C
In Dixieland where I was born in,
F
Early on one frosty mornin',
     C
Look away, look away,
     G7   C
Look away, Dixieland.

Refrain

           G7 C F
Then I wish I was in Dixie,
     D7   G7
Hooray! Hooray!
    C   G7 C F
In Dixieland I'll make my stand,
    C   G G7
To live and die in Dixie;
    C   G7
Away, away,
    C   G7 C
Away down south in Dixie;
     G7
Away, away,
    C   G7 C
Away down south in Dixie.

Copyright © 2008 Amsco Publications, a Division of Music Sales Corporation.
All Rights Reserved. International Copyright Secured.

Cripple Creek

Traditional

Verse 1

   D   G   D
I got a gal at the head of the creek;
                    A7   D
Go up to see her 'bout the middle of the week.
                       G   D
Kiss her on the mouth, just as sweet as any wine;
                       A7   D
Wraps herself around her, like a sweet pertater vine.

Chorus

   D
Goin' up Cripple Creek, goin' in a run,
                  A7   D
Goin' up Cripple Creek, have a little fun.

Goin' up Cripple Creek, goin' in a whirl,
                  A7   D
Goin' up Cripple Creek to see my girl.

Verse 2

   D   G   D
Girls on the Cripple Creek, 'bout half-grown,
               A7   D
Jump on a boy like a dog on a bone.
            G   D
Roll my britches up to my knees;
                  A7   D
I'll wade old Cripple Creek when I please.

Chorus

   D
Goin' up Cripple Creek, goin' in a run,
                  A7   D
Goin' up Cripple Creek, have a little fun.

Goin' up Cripple Creek, goin' in a whirl,
                  A7   D
Goin' up Cripple Creek to see my girl.

Copyright © 2008 Amsco Publications, a Division of Music Sales Corporation.
All Rights Reserved. International Copyright Secured.

Verse 3

D   **G**   **D**
Cripple Creek's wide and Cripple Creek's deep,
                      A7   **D**
I'll wade ol' Cripple Creek afore I sleep.
                G   **D**
Roads are rocky and hillside's muddy,
                   A7   **D**
And I'm so drunk that I can't stand steady.

Chorus

D
Goin' up Cripple Creek, goin' in a run,
                     A7   **D**
Goin' up Cripple Creek, have a little fun.

Goin' up Cripple Creek, goin' in a whirl,
                     A7   **D**
Goin' up Cripple Creek to see my girl.

Cumberland Gap

Traditional

Verse 1

D   Bm
Me an' my wife an' my wife's pap,
D   G   D
We all live down in Cumberland Gap.
D   Bm
Cumberland Gap is a noted place,
    D   G   D
Three kinds of water to wash your face.

Chorus

D   Bm
Cumberland Gap, Cumberland Gap.
D   G
Way down yonder in Cumberland Gap.
                   Bm
Cumberland Gap, Cumberland Gap.
D   G
Way down yonder in Cumberland Gap.

Verse 2

D   Bm
First white man in Cumberland Gap,
    D   G   D
Was Doctor Walker, an English chap.
                 Bm
Daniel Boone on Pinnacle Rock,
D   G   D
He killed Indians with his old flintlock.

Copyright © 2008 Amsco Publications, a Division of Music Sales Corporation.
All Rights Reserved. International Copyright Secured.

Chorus

D　　　　　　　　　　　　**Bm**
Cumberland Gap, Cumberland Gap.
D　　　　　　　　　　　**G**
Way down yonder in Cumberland Gap.
　　　　　　　　　　　　　Bm
Cumberland Gap, Cumberland Gap.
D　　　　　　　　　　　　**G**
Way down yonder in Cumberland Gap.

Verse 3

D　　　　　　　　　　　　**Bm**
Cumberland Gap with its cliffs an' rocks,
D　　　　　　　**G**　　　**D**
Home of the panther, bear an' fox.
D　　　　　　　　　　　**Bm**
Lay down boys an' take a little nap,
D　　　　　　**G**　　　　**D**
Fo'teen miles to Cumberland Gap.

Chorus

D　　　　　　　　　　　　**Bm**
Cumberland Gap, Cumberland Gap.
D　　　　　　　　　　　**G**
Way down yonder in Cumberland Gap.
　　　　　　　　　　　　　Bm
Cumberland Gap, Cumberland Gap.
D　　　　　　　　　　　　**G**
Way down yonder in Cumberland Gap.

Danny Boy

Traditional

Intro

| C | C7 | F | |
| Fm | C | G7 | |

Verse 1

             C   C7   F
Oh Danny boy, the pipes, the pipes are calling,
     Fm   C   Am   G7
From glen to glen, and down the mountain side.
             C   C7 F
The summer's gone, and all the roses falling,
   Fm   C/G   G7   C
It's you, it's you must go and I must bide.

Chorus 1

           C
But come ye back;
     F   G7 C
When summer's in the meadow,
  G7   Am   F
Or when the valley's hushed,
   C/E   D7
And white with snow.
G7   C   F
   'Tis I'll be there in sunshine
F♯°   C/G E7 Am
Or in sha––— dow,
  Fm C/G Am F   G7   C
Oh Danny boy, oh Danny boy, I love you so!

Link

| C | C7 | F | |
| Fm | C | G7 | |

Copyright © 2008 Amsco Publications, a Division of Music Sales Corporation.
All Rights Reserved. International Copyright Secured.

Verse 2

       C   **C7**   **F**
But if he come, when all the flow'rs are dying,
  Fm C   **Am**   **G7**
And I am dead, as dead I well may be.
              C   **C7 F**
Ye'll come and find the place where I am lying,
  Fm   **C/G** **G7**   **C**
And kneel and say an "Ave" there for me.

Chorus 2

         C   **F**   **G7**   **C**
And I shall hear, tho' soft your tread above me,
G7   **Am**   **F**   **C/E**   **D7**
  And all my dreams will warm and sweeter be.
G7   **C**   **F**
  If you'll not fail to tell me.
F#°   **C/G E7 Am**
That you lo– –ve me,
  Fm   **C/G** **Am**   **F**   **G7**   **Am**
Then I shall sleep in peace until you come to me.
Fm   **C/G**   **Am**   **F**   **G7**   **C**
I'll simply sleep in peace until you come to me.

Down In The Valley

Traditional

Verse 1

   D7   **G**   **D**
Down in the valley, valley so low,
        D7   **G**
Late in the evening, hear the train blow.
                          D
Hear the train blowing, hear that train blow;
             Am D7   **G**
Hang your head over, hear that train blow.

Verse 2

   D7   **G**   **D**
Roses love sunshine, violets love dew,
        D7   **G**
Angels in heaven know I love you.
                         D
Know I love you, dear, know I love you,
          Am   **D7**   **G**
Angels in heaven know I love you.

Verse 3

   D7   **G**   **D**
Write me a letter, send it by mail,
        D7   **G**
Send it in care of the Birmingham jail.
                         D
Birmingham jail house, Birmingham jail,
          Am   **D7**   **G**
Send it in care of the Birmingham jail.

Copyright © 2008 Amsco Publications, a Division of Music Sales Corporation.
All Rights Reserved. International Copyright Secured.

Verse 4

    D7   **G**   **D**
If you don't love me, love whom you please,
                   D7   **G**
Throw your arms 'round me, give my heart ease.
                           D
Give my heart ease, love, give my heart ease,
             Am   **D7**   **G**
Throw your arms 'round me, give my heart ease.

Verse 5

    D7   **G**   **D**
Down in the valley, valley so low,
          D7   **G**
Late in the evening, hear the wind blow.
                        D
Hear the wind blowing, hear that wind blow;
          Am **D7**   **G**
Hang your head over, hear that wind blow.

The First Noel

Traditional

Verse 1

D A7   D A7 G♯° D
The first Noel, the an - gel did say,
    A7 G♯° D   G   A7 D   A7 D
Was to certain poor shepherds in fields as they lay,
          A7   D   A7 G♯° D
In fields where they lay keeping their sheep,
    A7 G♯° D   G A7 D   A7 D
On a cold win - ter's night__ that was so deep.

Refrain

D Bm F♯m G G♯° D A7
Noel, No - el, Noel, Noel,_____
D   A7 G♯° D   G A7 D A7 D
Born is   the   King__ of Is - ra - el!

Verse 2

D   A7   D A7 G♯° D
They looked up and saw_____ a   star,
        A7 G♯° D   G A7 D   A7 D
Shining in___ the East__ be - yond them far,
      D   A7   D A7 G♯°   D
And to the earth it gave___ great light,
       A7 G♯° D   G A7 D   A7 D
And so it   con - tin - ued both day and night.

Refrain

D Bm F♯m G G♯° D A7
Noel, No - el, Noel, Noel,_____
D   A7 G♯° D   G A7 D A7 D
Born is   the   King__ of Is - ra - el!

Copyright © 2008 Amsco Publications, a Division of Music Sales Corporation.
All Rights Reserved. International Copyright Secured.

Verse 3

   D **A7** **D** **A7 G♯° D**
And by the light of that___ same star,
    A7 G♯° D **G** **A7** **D** **A7 D**
Three wise___ men came__ from country far,
     A7 D **A7 G♯° D**
To seek for a King was their in - tent,
     A7 G♯° D **G A7 D** **A7 D**
And to follow the star__ wherever it went.

Refrain

   D **Bm F♯m G G♯° D** **A7**
Noel, No - el, Noel, Noel,_____
   D **A7 G♯° D** **G A7 D** **A7 D**
Born is the King__ of Is - ra - el!

Verse 4

     A7 **D A7 G♯° D**
This star drew nigh to the___ northwest,
    A7 G♯° D **G A7 D** **A7 D**
O'er Beth - le - hem__ it took its rest,
    A7 D **A7** **G♯° D**
And there it did both pause and stay,
    A7 G♯° D **G A7** **D A7 D**
Right o'er the place_ where Jesus lay.

Refrain

   D **Bm F♯m G G♯° D** **A7**
Noel, No - el, Noel, Noel,_____
   D **A7 G♯° D** **G A7 D A7 D**
Born is the King__ of Is - ra - el!

Verse 5

        A7 D   A7 G♯° D
Then entered in those wise men three,
    A7 G♯° D G A7 D A7 D
Full rev'rent - ly__ up - on their knee,
        A7 D A7 G♯° D
And offered there in His pres - ence,
     A7 G♯° D   G A7 D   A7 D
Their gold and myrrh __and frankin - cense.

Refrain

    D Bm F♯m G G♯° D A7
Noel, No - el, Noel, Noel,_____
D   A7 G♯° D G A7 D A7 D
Born is the King__ of Is - ra - el!

Verse 6

        A7 D   A7 G♯° D
Then let us all with one ac - cord,
    A7 G♯° D G A7 D A7 D
Sing praises to our heavenly Lord,
           A7   D A7 G♯° D
That hath made Heaven and earth of naught,
    A7 G♯° D   G A7 D   A7 D
And with his blood__ mankind has bought.

Refrain

    D Bm F♯m G G♯° D A7
Noel, No - el, Noel, Noel,_____
D   A7 G♯° D G A7 D A7 D
Born is the King__ of Is - ra - el!

Flag Of The Free

Words by J.P. McCaskey
Music by Richard Wagner
"Bridal Chorus" from Lohengrin

Verse 1

A   E7 A
Flag of the free! Fairest to see!
        D/A A   B7   E
Borne through the strife and the thunder of war,
A   E   A
Banner so bright with starry light,
       C#m F#m Bm E7 A
Float ever proud - ly from mountain to shore.
D/A   Bm   E A/E E
Sages of old thy coming foresaw,
D/A   Bm   F# C#   F#
Empire of justice, empire of law;
      B/F# F# B/F# C#7
Flag of   our fathers! Round all the world,
F#   D#m   G#7   C#7
Blest of the millions, whenever unfurled;
F#m A/E E   E7 A
Terror to tyrants, hope to the slave,
      F#m C#m F#m C#m G#7 C#   E
Spread thy fair folds to   shield and to save.__

Refrain

A   E   A
Flag of the free, all hail to thee!
     D/A A   B7   E
Floating the fairest on ocean or shore,
A   E7 A
Loud ring the cry, ne'er let it die,
      C#m F#m Bm E7 A
"Union and Lib - erty now, evermore!"

Copyright © 2008 Amsco Publications, a Division of Music Sales Corporation.
All Rights Reserved. International Copyright Secured.

Verse 2

A   E7 A
Flag of the free! All turn to thee,
     D/A A B7   E
Golden thy stars in the blue of their sky!
A   E A
Flag of the brave! Onward to save,
A   E A
Crimson thy bars float gaily on high!
     C♯m F♯m Bm E7 A
Splendid thy sto - ry, mighty to save,
D/A   Bm   E A/E E
Matchless thy beauty on land or wave,
D/A   Bm   F♯ C♯ F♯
Heroes have borne thee aloft in the fray,
  B/F♯ F♯ B/F♯   C♯7
Foemen who scorn thee have all pass'd away;
F♯m A/E E E7 A
Pride of our country, hail'd from afar,
  F♯m C♯m F♯m C♯m G♯7 C♯ E
Banner of prom - ise, lose not a star.____

Refrain

A   E A
Flag of the free, all hail to thee!
    D/A A B7 E
Floating the fairest on ocean or shore,
A   E7 A
Loud ring the cry, ne'er let it die,
    C♯m F♯m Bm E7 A
"Union and Lib - erty now, evermore!"

```
A                       E7    A
```
Flag of the brave, long may it wave!
```
        D/A  A          B7            E
```
Chosen of God while His might we adore,
```
A               E           A
```
High in the van, for manhood of man,
```
        C♯m  F♯m       Bm  E7     A
```
Symbol of right through the years passing o'er;
```
D/A         Bm     E    A/E   E
```
Flow'r of the ages,   promised of yore,
```
D/A            Bm  E   A/E  E
```
Flow'r of the ages, fade nevermore!
```
     B/F♯  F♯  B/F♯     C♯7
```
Emblem of   freedom, "Many in One,"
```
F♯            D♯m  G♯7      C♯7
```
O'er thee thine eagle, bird of the sun;
```
F♯m        A/E      E     E7      A
```
All hail "Old Glory!" hearts leap to see,
```
     F♯m  C♯m  F♯m    C♯m  G♯7    C♯   E
```
How from na - tions the world looks to thee.__

```
A               E    A
```
Flag of the free, all hail to thee!
```
        D/A   A    B7     E
```
Floating the fairest on ocean or shore,
```
A                 E7  A
```
Loud ring the cry, ne'er let it die,
```
        C♯m  F♯m  Bm  E7 A
```
"Union and Lib - erty   now, evermore!"

For He's A Jolly Good Fellow

Traditional

```
     F                C7  F
For he's a jolly good fel - low,
  C7              F
For he's a jolly good fellow,
                   B♭  A♭°7
For he's a jolly good fel - low,
     F/C    C7    F7
Which nobody can deny,
                B♭   F
Which nobody can deny,
                B♭   F
Which nobody can deny,
                   B♭  D°
For he's a jolly good fel - low,
     F/C    C7    F
Which nobody can deny,
```

Copyright © 2008 Amsco Publications, a Division of Music Sales Corporation.
All Rights Reserved. International Copyright Secured.

Give My Regards To Broadway

Words and Music by George M. Cohan

B♭ **Cm7 F7**
Give my regards to Broadway,
 Cm7 **F7** **B♭**
Remember me to Herald Square,
 F/C C7 Dm7
Tell all the gang at For - ty Second Street
Gm **C7** **F7**
That I will soon be there,
B♭ **Cm7 F7**
Whisper of how I'm yearning
Cm7 **F7** **B♭**
To mingle with the old time throng,
G7 **Cm G** **Cm7**
Give my regards to old Broadway
 B♭/F Gm Cm7 F7 B♭
And say that I'll be there, e'er long,

Copyright © 2008 Amsco Publications, a Division of Music Sales Corporation.
All Rights Reserved. International Copyright Secured.

Give Me That Old Time Religion

Traditional

                A
Verse 1   Give me that old time religion,
             E7   **A**
           Give me that old time religion,
             A7   **D**
           Give me that old time religion,
           A   **E7**   **A**
           It's good enough for me.

Verse 2   It was good for our fathers.
           E7
           It was good for our fathers.
           A7   **D**
           It was good for our fathers.
           A   **E7**   **A**
           And it's good enough for me.

Verse 3   It was good for our mothers.
           E7
           It was good for our mothers.
           A7   **D**
           It was good for our mothers.
           A   **E7**   **A**
           And it's good enough for me.

Copyright © 2008 Amsco Publications, a Division of Music Sales Corporation.
All Rights Reserved. International Copyright Secured.

Verse 4

Makes me love everybody.
       E7   **A**
Makes me love everybody.
       A7   **D**
Makes me love everybody.
    A   **E7**   **A**
And it's good enough for me.

Verse 5

It will take us all to heaven.
      E7   **A**
It will take us all to heaven.
     A7   **D**
It will take us all to heaven.
    A   **E7**   **A**
And it's good enough for me.

      A

Verse 6

Give me that old time religion,
       E7   **A**
Give me that old time religion,
       A7   **D**
Give me that old time religion,
  A   **E7**   **A**
It's good enough for me.

Go Tell It On The Mountain

Traditional

Chorus

G C   G
Go, tell it on the mountain,
D   C   G
Over the hills and everywhere;
   C   G Em
Go, tell it on the mountain,
   Am   D G
That Jesus Christ is born.

Verse 1

G
While shepherds kept their watching
   D   Em D G
Over silent flocks by night,

Behold throughout the heavens,
   A7   D D7
There shone a holy light.

Chorus

Verse 2

     G
The shepherds feared and trembled,
   D   Em D G
When lo! above the earth,

Rang out the angels chorus,
   A7   D D7
That hailed the Savior's birth.

Chorus

Copyright © 2008 Amsco Publications, a Division of Music Sales Corporation.
All Rights Reserved. International Copyright Secured.

Verse 3

   G
Down in a lowly manger,
   D   **Em** **D** **G**
The humble Christ was born,

And God sent us salvation,
   A7   **D** **D7**
That blessed Christmas morn.

Chorus

Verse 4

   G
I too am like a shepherd,
   D   **Em D G**
My flock of days to guard,

Each day finds time for praying,
   A7   **D**   **D7**
From this I won't retard.

Chorus

G C   **G**
Go, tell it on the mountain,
D   **C**   **G**
Over the hills and everywhere;
   C   **G** **Em**
Go, tell it on the mountain,
   Am   **D G**
That Jesus Christ is born.

God Of Our Fathers

Words by Daniel C. Roberts
Music by George W. Warren

Verse 1

D   Bm A/C# D G/B D/A   Asus4 A7 D
God of   our   fa - thers, Whose almight - y   hand,
      Bm   F#m B7 A/E Esus4 E A
Leads forth in beau - ty all the star - ry band,
              F   F7 Am/E Esus4 E A
Of shining worlds in splendor through the skies,
D/F# G   D   B7 Em D   Asus4 A7 D
Our grateful songs be - fore Thy throne a - rise.

Verse 2

D   Bm A/C# D G/B D/A Asus4 A7 D
Thy love di - vine hath led us in   the past,
      Bm   F#m B7 A/E   Esus4 E A
In this free land by Thee our lot   is cast,
              F   F7 Am/E   Esus4 E A
Be Thou our Ru - ler, Guardian, Guide and Stay,
D/F# G   D   B7 Em D   Asus4 A7 D
Thy Word our law, Thy paths our chos - en way.

Verse 3

D   Bm   A/C# D   G/B D/A Asus4 A7 D
From war's a - larms, from deadly pest - il - ence,
      Bm   F#m B7 A/E Esus4 E A
Be Thy strong arm our ever sure de - fense;
          F   F7 Am/E Esus4 E A
Thy true religion in our   hearts in - crease,
D/F# G   D   B7 Em D   Asus4 A7 D
Thy bounteous goodness nourish us   in peace.

Verse 4

D Bm A/C# D G/B D/A   Asus4 A7   D
Refresh Thy people   on their toil - some way,
      Bm   F#m B7 A/E Esus4 E A
Lead us from night to never end - ing day;
          F   F7 Am/E Esus4 E A
Fill all our lives with love and grace di - vine,
D/F# G   D   B7 Em D Asus4 A7 D
And glory, laud, and praise be ev - er Thine.

Copyright © 2008 Amsco Publications, a Division of Music Sales Corporation.
All Rights Reserved. International Copyright Secured.

Goodbye, My Lady Love

Words and Music by Joe E. Howard

F
Goodbye, my lady love,

Farewell, my turtle dove,
G7   **C7**   **F**   **F°7** **F**
You are the idol and darling of my heart,

But some day you will come back to me,

And love me tenderly,
  G7   **C7**   **F** **C7** **F**
So goodbye, my lady love, goodbye._____

Copyright © 2008 Amsco Publications, a Division of Music Sales Corporation.
All Rights Reserved. International Copyright Secured.

God Save America

Words by William G. Ballantine
Music by Alexis F. Lvov

Verse 1

| D | G | D | | G | A7sus4 G | D | B |

God save America! New world of glo - ry,

Em A   **D**   **Bm F#m C#7**   **F#m**

Newborn to freedom and knowledge and power,

A7   **D**   **F#7 Bm Em Bm F#7 G F#m**

Lifting the towers of her light - ning-lit ci - ties,

Bm   **Dmaj7 G**   **D**   **B9 Esus4**   **Em D**   **Asus4 A7 D**

Where the   flood tides___ of   hu - man - i -   ty roar!

Verse 2

D   **G**   **D**   **G**   **A7sus4 G**   **D**   **B**

God save America! Here may   all rac - es,

Em A   **D**   **Bm F#m C#7 F#m**

Mingle together as child - ren of   God,

A7   **D**   **F#7 Bm Em Bm F#7 G F#m**

Founding an empire of bro - ther - ly kindness,

Bm Dmaj7 G D B9 Esus4 Em D   **Asus4 A7 D**

Eq - ual   in li - ber - ty, made of   one blood!

Verse 3

D   **G**   **D**   **G A7sus4 G**   **D**   **B**

God save America! Brother -   hood ban - ish,

Em A   **D**   **Bm F#m C#7**   **F#m**

Wail of the worker and curse of the crushed;

A7   **D**   **F#7 Bm Em Bm F#7 G F#m**

Joy break in songs from her ju   -   bi - lant millions,

Bm   **Dmaj7 G D B9 Esus4 Em D Asus4 A7 D**

Hail - ing   the day___ when_____ discords   are hushed!

Copyright © 2008 Amsco Publications, a Division of Music Sales Corporation.
All Rights Reserved. International Copyright Secured.

Verse 4

D	G	D		G	A7sus4 G D	B

God save America! Bearing   the ol - ive,

| Em | A | D | | Bm | F#m | C#7 | F#m |

Hers be the blessing the   peacemakers prove,

| A7 | D | | F#7 Bm Em | Bm | F#7 G | F#m |

Calling the nations to   glad_____ fe - der - a - tions,

| Bm Dmaj7 G D | B9 Esus4 | Em D | Asus4 A7 D |

Leading   the world___ in   the tri - umph of love!

Verse 5

| D | G | D | | G | A7sus4 G D | B |

God save America! 'Mid all   her splendors;

| Em | A | D | | Bm | F#m C#7 | F#m |

Save her from pride and   luxu - ry;

| A7 | D | | F#7 Bm Em | Bm F#7 G | F#m |

Throne in her heart and un - seen e - ter - nal;

| Bm Dmaj7 G D | B9 Esus4 | Em D | Asus4 A7 D |

Right be   her might__ and   the truth make her free!

Goodnight, Ladies

Words and Music by E.P. Christy

Verse 1

G
Goodnight, ladies!
        D/F♯
Goodnight, ladies!
G   **G7**
Goodnight, ladies!
       C   **D7**   **G**
We're going to leave you now.

Refrain

G
Merrily we roll along,
D7/F♯ D7 G
Roll   along, roll along,

Merrily we roll along,
D7/F♯   **D7**   **G**
Over the deep blue sea.

Verse 2

G
Farewell, ladies!
        D/F♯
Farewell, ladies!
G   **G7**
Farewell, ladies!
       C   **D7**   **G**
We're going to leave you now.

Refrain

G
Merrily we roll along,
D7/F♯ D7 G
Roll   along, roll along,

Merrily we roll along,
D7/F♯   **D7**   **G**
Over the deep blue sea.

Copyright © 2008 Amsco Publications, a Division of Music Sales Corporation.
All Rights Reserved. International Copyright Secured.

Verse 3

G
Sweet dreams, ladies!
         D/F♯
Sweet dreams, ladies!
G   **G7**
Sweet dreams, ladies!
      C   **D7**   **G**
We're going to leave you now.

Refrain

G
Merrily we roll along,
D7/F♯ D7 G
Roll   along, roll along,

Merrily we roll along,
D7/F♯ D7   **G**
Over the deep blue sea.

Verse 4

G
Goodnight, ladies!
         D/F♯
Goodnight, ladies!
G   **G7**
Goodnight, ladies!
      C   **D7**   **G**
We're going to leave you now.

Hail, Columbia

Words by Joseph Hopkinson
Music by Philip Phile

Verse 1

G   D   G
Hail Columbia, happy land!
         D7   G
Hail, ye her - oes, heav'n-born band,
                      D7   G
Who fought and bled in freedom's cause,
                      D7   G
Who fought and bled in freedom's cause,
    D/F♯ A7/E D   A7   D
And when the   storm of war was gone
A7 D   Em D/A A7 D
En - joyed the peace your valor won.
       G/D D7 G/D D7
Let inde - pendence be our boast,
D   G   D
Ever mindful what it cost,
       G   D   G
Ever grateful for the prize,
      D7   G
Let its altar reach the skies.

Refrain

            D7   G
Firm, united let us be,
                D7 G
Rallying round our liberty,
Am   D7 G
As a band of brothers joined,
     C G/D D7 G
Peace and safe - ty we shall find.

Copyright © 2008 Amsco Publications, a Division of Music Sales Corporation.
All Rights Reserved. International Copyright Secured.

Verse 2

G   **D**   **G**

Immortal patriots, rise once more,

          D7   **G**

Defend your rights,   defend your shore!

             D7   **G**

Let no rude foe, with impious hand,

             D7   **G**

Let no rude foe, with impious hand,

D/F♯ A7/E D   **A7**   **D**

Invade the   shrine where sacred lies

A7 **D** **Em D/A**   **A7 D**

Of   toil and blood, the well-earned prize,

    G/D   **D7**   **G/D D7**

While off'ring peace, sin - cere and just,

   D   **G**   **D**

In Heav'n we place a manly trust,

         G D G

That truth and justice will prevail,

       D7   **G**

And every scheme of bondage fail.

Refrain

         D7   **G**

Firm, united let us be,

            D7 G

Rallying round our liberty,

Am   **D7 G**

As a band of brothers joined,

    C **G/D D7 G**

Peace and safe - ty   we shall find.

Verse 3

G   D   G
Sound, sound the trump of fame,
      D7   G
Let Washington's great fame,
                  D7   G
Ring through the world with loud applause,
                  D7   G
Ring through the world with loud applause,
D/F♯ A7/E D A7   D
Let ev'ry clime to freedom dear,
A7   D   Em D/A A7 D
Listen with a   joy - ful ear,
      G/D D7 G/D D7
With equal skill, with   God-like pow'r,
D   G   D
He governs in the fearful hour,
         G D G
Of horrid war, or guides with ease,
         D7   G
The happier time of honest peace.

Refrain

          D7 G
Firm, united let us be,
              D7 G
Rallying round our liberty,
Am   D7 G
As a band of brothers joined,
    C G/D D7 G
Peace and safe - ty we shall find.

Verse 4

       G   **D**   **G**
Behold the chief who now commands,
                  D7   **G**
Once more to serve   his country stands.
                  D7   **G**
The rock on which the storm will break,
                  D7   **G**
The rock on which the storm will break,
  D/F♯ **A7/E** **D**   **A7 D**
But armed in   virtue, firm, and true,
A7 **D**   **Em D/A**   **A7**   **D**
His hopes are fixed on Heav'n and you.
D   **G**   **D**
When glooms obscured Columbia's day,
    G   **D**   **G**
His steady mind, from changes free,
        D7   **G**
Resolved on death or liberty.

Refrain

           D7 **G**
Firm, united let us be,
              D7 **G**
Rallying round our liberty,
Am   **D7 G**
As a band of brothers joined,
      C **G/D** **D7 G**
Peace and safe - ty we shall find.

Hark! The Herald Angels Sing

Words by Charles Wesley
Music by Felix Mendelssohn

Verse 1

G   D G   D
Hark! The herald angels sing,__
G Bm C Am   C D7 G
Glory   to____ the newborn King;
            D Em G Em A7
Peace on earth and mer - cy mild,__
Bm A D   G A D
God and sinners reconciled;
          G D7 G   D
Joyful, all ye na - tions rise,
         G   D7 G   D
Join the triumph of the skies;_
C   Am E Am
With the angelic hosts proclaim,
D7   G   D7
Christ is born in Bethlehem.

Refrain

C   G Am E   Am
Hark! The herald an - gels sing
D D7 G   D7 G
Glory to the newborn King!

Verse 2

G   D G   D
Christ by highest heav'n adored;
G   Bm C Am C D7 G
Christ the ev - er - lasting Lord;
           D Em G Em A7
Late in time behold Him come,__
Bm A   D   G A D
Off - spring of a Virgin's womb.
         G D7 G   D
Veiled in flesh the Godhead see;
         G   D7 G D
Hail the incarnate De - i - ty,
C   Am E Am
Pleased as man with man to dwell,
D7   G D7
Jesus, our Emmanuel.

Copyright © 2008 Amsco Publications, a Division of Music Sales Corporation.
All Rights Reserved. International Copyright Secured.

Refrain

C   G Am E Am

Hark! The herald an - gels sing

D D7 G   D7 G

Glory to the newborn King!

Verse 3

G   D   G   D

Hail the heav'n-born Prince of Peace!

G Bm C Am C D7 G

Hail the Son of Righteousness!

D Em G Em A7

Light and life to all   He brings,__

Bm A   D   G A D

Ris'n with healing in His wings;

G D7 G   D

Mild He lays His glory by,

G D7 G   D

Born that man no more may die,

C   Am E Am

Born to raise the sons of earth,

D7   G   D7

Born to give them second birth.

Refrain

C   G Am E Am

Hark! The herald an - gels sing

D D7 G   D7 G

Glory to the newborn King!

He Leadeth Me

Words by Joseph H. Gilmore
Music by William B. Bradbury

Verse 1

         C   F/C
He leadeth me, O blessed thought!
         C   D7 G
O words with heavenly comfort fraught!
          C   F
Whate'er I do, where'er I be,
         C   F   C/G G7   C
Still 'tis God's hand that lead - eth me.

Refrain

            G7/D C/E F C
He leadeth me, He lead - eth me,
F C   F   C D7 G
By His own hand, He leadeth   me;
         C   G7/D C/E F   C
His faithful follower I   would be,
F C   F   C/G G7   C
For by His hand He lead - eth me.

Verse 2

         C   F/C
Sometimes 'mid scenes of deepest gloom,
         C   D7 G
Sometimes where Eden's bowers bloom,
         C   F
By waters still, over troubled sea,
         C   F   C/G G7   C
Still 'tis God's hand that lead - eth me.

Refrain

            G7/D C/E F C
He leadeth me, He lead - eth me,
F C   F   C D7 G
By His own hand, He leadeth   me;
         C   G7/D C/E F   C
His faithful follower I   would be,
F C   F   C/G G7   C
For by His hand He lead - eth me.

Copyright © 2008 Amsco Publications, a Division of Music Sales Corporation.
All Rights Reserved. International Copyright Secured.

Verse 3

        C   **F/C**
Lord, I would place my hand in Thine,
        C   **D7** **G**
Nor ever murmur nor re - pine;
        C   **F**
Content, whatever lot I see,
           C   **F**   **C/G G7** **C**
Since 'tis my God that lead - eth me.

Refrain

          G7/D **C/E** **F** **C**
He leadeth me, He lead - eth me,
F C   **F**   **C D7 G**
By His own hand, He leadeth me;
        C   **G7/D** **C/E F**   **C**
His faithful follower I   would be,
F C   **F**   **C/G G7** **C**
For by His hand He lead - eth me.

Verse 4

        C   **F/C**
And when my task on earth is done,
        C   **D7**   **G**
When by Thy grace the victory's won,
        C   **F**
E'en death's cold wave I will not flee,
        C   **F**   **C/G** **G7 C**
Since God through Jordan lead - eth me.

Refrain

          G7/D **C/E** **F** **C**
He leadeth me, He lead - eth me,
F C   **F**   **C D7 G**
By His own hand, He leadeth me;
        C   **G7/D** **C/E F**   **C**
His faithful follower I   would be,
F C   **F**   **C/G G7** **C**
For by His hand He lead - eth me.

He's Got The Whole World In His Hands

Traditional

Verse 1

         C
He's got the whole world in His hands,
         Dm7 G   **Dm7 G7**
He's got the whole world in His hands,
         C
He's got the whole world in His hands,
         G7   **C**
He's got the whole world in His hands.

Verse 2

He's got the tiny little baby in His hands,
         Dm7   **G**   **Dm7 G7**
He's got the tiny little baby in His hands,
         C
He's got the tiny little baby in His hands,
         G7   **C**
He's got the whole world in His hands.

Verse 3

He's got the wind and the rain in His hands,
         Dm7   **G**   **Dm7 G7**
He's got the wind and the rain in His hands,
         C
He's got the wind and the rain in His hands,
         G7   **C**
He's got the whole world in His hands.

Copyright © 2008 Amsco Publications, a Division of Music Sales Corporation.
All Rights Reserved. International Copyright Secured.

Verse 4

He's got you and me, brother, in His hands,
Dm7   **G**   **Dm7 G7**
He's got you and me, brother, in His hands,
C
He's got you and me, brother, in His hands,
G7   **C**
He's got the whole world in His hands.

Verse 5

He's got ev'rybody here in His hands.
Dm7   **G**   **Dm7 G7**
He's got ev'rybody here in His hands,
C
He's got ev'rybody here in His hands,
G7   **C**
He's got the whole world in His hands.

C

Verse 6

He's got the whole world in His hands,
Dm7 G   **Dm7 G7**
He's got the whole world in His hands,
C
He's got the whole world in His hands,
G7   **C**
He's got the whole world in His hands.

Holy, Holy, Holy

Words by Reginald Heber
Music by John B. Dykes

Verse 1

F   Dm C F
Holy, holy, ho - ly!
B♭   F
Lord God almighty!
C   F C G7 C
Early in the morning,
F   C   G7   C7
Our song shall rise to thee;
F   Dm C F
Holy, holy, ho - ly,
B♭   F
Merciful and mighty!
Dm F F7 Dm F F7 B♭   C7 F
God in three per - sons,__ blessed trinity!

Verse 2

F   Dm C F
Holy, holy, ho - ly!
B♭   F
All the saints adore Thee,
C   F   C G7   C
Casting down their golden crowns,
F C   G7   C7
A - round the glassy sea,
F   Dm   C F
Cherubim and seraphim,
F   Dm   C F
Falling down before Thee,
Dm F   F7 Dm F F7 B♭ C7 F
Who wert and art, and evermore shall be.

Copyright © 2008 Amsco Publications, a Division of Music Sales Corporation.
All Rights Reserved. International Copyright Secured.

Verse 3

F   Dm C F
Holy, holy, ho - ly!
B♭   F
Though the darkness hide Thee,
C   F C G7 C
Though the eye of sinful man,
F   C   G7   C7
Thy glory may not see;
F   Dm   C   F
Only thou art ho - ly,
B♭   F
There is none beside thee,
Dm F F7 Dm F F7 B♭   C7 F
Per - fect in pow - er,___ love, and purity.

Verse 4

F   Dm C F
Holy, holy, ho - ly!
B♭   F
Lord God almighty!
C   F   C   G7   C
All thy works shall praise thy name,
F C   G7   C7
In earth, and sky, and sea;
F   Dm C F
Holy, holy, ho - ly!
B♭   F
Merciful and mighty!
Dm F F7   Dm F F7 B♭   C7 F
God in three per - sons,___ blessed trinity!

Home Again From A Foreign Shore

Words and Music by Marshall S. Pike

Verse 1

E
Home again, home again,
A   E   B
From a foreign shore!
     E   A
And oh, it fills my soul with joy,
     E/B   B7   E
To meet my friends once more.
B   E
Here I dropped my parting tear,
     A   B   E
To cross the ocean's foam,
                              A
But now I'm once again with those,
     E/B   B7   A
Who kindly greet me home.

Refrain

E
Home again, home again,
A   E   B
From a foreign shore!
     E   A
And oh, it fills my soul with joy,
     E/B   B7   E
To meet my friends once more.

Verse 2

E
Happy hearts, happy hearts,
     A   E   B
With mine have laughed with glee,
     E   A
And oh, the friends I loved in youth,
     E/B B7 E
Seem happier to me;
B   E
And if my guide should be my fate,
     A   B   E
Which bids me longer roam,
                        A
But death alone can break the tie,
     E/B   B7   A
That binds my heart to home.

Copyright © 2008 Amsco Publications, a Division of Music Sales Corporation.
All Rights Reserved. International Copyright Secured.

Refrain
       E
Home again, home again,
A   **E**   **B**
From a foreign shore!
    E   **A**
And oh, it fills my soul with joy,
    E/B   **B7**   **E**
To meet my friends once more.

Verse 3
       E
Music sweet, music soft,
A   **E**   **B**
Lingers round the place,
    E   **A**
And oh, I feel the childhood charm,
    E/B   **B7** **E**
That time cannot efface.
     B   **E**
Then give me but my homestead roof,
     A   **B**   **E**
I'll ask no palace dome,
                A
For I can live a happy life,
    E/B   **B7**   **A**
With those I love at home.

Refrain
       E
Home again, home again,
A   **E**   **B**
From a foreign shore!
    E   **A**
And oh, it fills my soul with joy,
    E/B   **B7**   **E**
To meet my friends once more.

Home On The Range

Traditional

Verse 1

G   C
Oh, give me a home where the buffalo roam,
          G   A7   D7
Where the deer and the antelope play.
   G   C
Where seldom is heard a discouraging word,
       G   D7   G
And the skies are not cloudy all day.

Chorus

    D7   G
Home, home on the range,
        Em   A7   D
Where the deer and the antelope play.
   G   C   Cm
Where seldom is heard a discouraging word,
       G   D7   G
And the skies are not cloudy all day.

Verse 2

         G   C
How often at night where the heavens are bright,
        G   A7   D7
With the light of the glittering stars.
     G   C
Have I stood there amazed and asked as I gazed,
     G   D7   G
If their glory exceeds that of ours.

Chorus

Verse 3

         G   C
Where the air is so pure, the zephyr's so free,
     G   A7   D7
The breezes so balmy and light.
     G   C
That I would not exchange my home on the range,
     G   D7   G
For all of the cities so bright.

Copyright © 2008 Amsco Publications, a Division of Music Sales Corporation.
All Rights Reserved. International Copyright Secured.

Chorus

Verse 4
     G
Oh, I love those wild flowers,
     C
In this dear land of ours,
  G   **A7**   **D7**
The curlew, I love to hear scream.
    G   **C**
And I love the white rocks and the antelope flocks,
   G   **D7**   **G**
That graze on the mountain tops green.

Chorus

Verse 5
    G   **C**
Then give me a land where the bright diamond sand,
   G   **A7**   **D7**
Flows leisurely down to the stream.
      G   **C**
Where the graceful white swan goes gliding along,
   G   **D7**   **G**
Like a maid in a heavenly dream.

Chorus
   D7   **G**
Home, home on the range,
      Em   **A7**   **D**
Where the deer and the antelope play.
   G   **C**   **Cm**
Where seldom is heard a discouraging word,
   G   **D7**   **G**
And the skies are not cloudy all day.

Hail To The Chief

Words by Sir Walter Scott
Music by James Sanderson

Intro   ‖: C | :‖

Verse

     C   F
‖: Hail to the chief,
                  G7 C
Who in triumph advan - ces,
                        D7   G7
Honored and blessed be the evergreen pine!
C   F/C   C   G7 C
Long may the tree in his banner that glances,
            F C   G7   C
Flourish the shelter and grace of our line,

Heav'n send it happy dew,
Dm   G
Earth lend it sap anew;
C   G7 C/G F   C G7
Gaily to burgeon and   broadly to grow.
C
While every highland glen,
Dm   F
Send our shout back again,
C
"Roderigh Alpine dhu ho! Ieroe!" :‖

Copyright © 2008 Amsco Publications, a Division of Music Sales Corporation.
All Rights Reserved. International Copyright Secured.

Home, Sweet Home

Words and Music by Henry R. Bishop

Verse 1

      F C7   F   C7   F
'Mid pleasures and palaces, though we may roam,
        C7 F   C7   F
Be it ever so humble, there's no place like home.
           Bb   F   C7   F
A charm from the skies seems to hallow us there,
               Bb   C7   F
Which, seek through the world, is ne'er met with elsewhere.

Refrain

        Gm
Home, home,
F/C C7 F
Home, sweet home.
          Bb   F
There's no place like home,
        C7   F
There's no place like home.

Verse 2

      F C7 F   C7   F
I gaze on the moon as I tread the drear wild,
          C7   F   C7   F
And feel that my mother now thinks of her child,
           Bb   F   C7   F
As she looks on the moon from our own cottage door,
             Bb   C7   F
Through the woodbine whose fragrance shall cheer me no more.

Refrain

        Gm
Home, home,
F/C C7 F
Home, sweet home.
          Bb   F
There's no place like home,
        C7   F
There's no place like home.

Copyright © 2008 Amsco Publications, a Division of Music Sales Corporation.
All Rights Reserved. International Copyright Secured.

Verse 3

   F C7 **F**   **C7**   **F**
An exile from home, splendor dazzles in vain,
 C7   **F**   **C7**   **F**
Oh, give me my low, thatched cottage again,
  B♭   **F**   **C7**   **F**
The birds singing gaily that come at my call,
       B♭   **C7**   **F**
Give me them, and that peace of mind, dearer than all.

Refrain

   Gm
Home, home,
F/C **C7** **F**
Home, sweet home.
    B♭   **F**
There's no place like home,
   C7   **F**
There's no place like home.

Verse 4

    F **C7 F** **C7**   **F**
How sweet 'tis to sit 'neath a fond father's smile,
    C7   **F**   **C7**   **F**
And the cares of a mother to soothe and beguile.
  B♭   **F**   **C7**   **F**
Let others delight 'mid new pleasures to roam,
    B♭   **C7**   **F**
But give me, oh, give me the pleasures of home.

Refrain

   Gm
Home, home,
F/C **C7** **F**
Home, sweet home.
    B♭   **F**
There's no place like home,
   C7   **F**
There's no place like home.

Verse 5

       F **C7** **F**   **C7**   **F**
To thee I'll return overburdened with care,
  C7   **F**   **C7**   **F**
The heart's dearest solace will smile on me there,
  B♭   **F**   **C7**   **F**
No more from that cottage again will I roam,
    B♭   **C7**   **F**
Be it ever so humble, there's no place like home.

Refrain

      Gm
Home, home,
F/C **C7** **F**
Home, sweet home.
        B♭   **F**
There's no place like home,
      C7   **F**
There's no place like home.

House Of The Rising Sun

Traditional

Verse 1

Am D7   E7   Am
There is a house in New Orleans,
               G7   C
They call the Rising Sun.
E7   Am   Am7 D/A   F7
   And it's been the ruin of many a poor girl,
   Am E7   Am
And I, oh Lord, was one.

Verse 2

E7 Am D7   E7   Am
  If I had listened to what mama had said,
              G7   C
I'd have been at home today,
E7   Am   Am7   D/A F7
  Being so young and foolish, poor girl,
    Am   F7   Am
Let a gambler lead me astray.

Verse 3

E7   Am   D7 E7 Am
  My mother she's a tail–or,
             G7   C
She sells those new blue jeans.
E7   Am   Am7 D/A   F7
  My sweetheart, he's a drunk–ard,
Am   E7   Am
Lord, down in New Orleans.

Verse 4

E7   Am D7   E7   Am
  Now the only thing a drunkard needs,
            G7   C
Is a suitcase and a trunk.
E7   Am Am7   D/A F7
  And the only time he's satis–fied,
    Am   E7 Am
Is when he's on a drunk.

Copyright © 2008 Amsco Publications, a Division of Music Sales Corporation.
All Rights Reserved. International Copyright Secured.

Verse 5

    E7   Am   D7 E7 Am
      Go tell my baby sis–ter,
             G7   C
Never do what I have done,
E7   Am   Am7   D/A   F7
      To shun that house in New Orleans,
      Am   E7   Am
They call the Rising Sun.

Verse 6

    E7   Am D7   E7   Am
      One foot is on the plat–form,
           G7   C
And the other is on the train.
E7   Am Am7   D/A   F7
      I'm goin' back to New Orleans,
    Am   E7   Am
To wear that ball and chain.

Verse 7

    E7   Am D7   E7   Am
      I'm going back to New Orleans,
         G7   C
My race is almost won.
E7 Am Am7   D/A   F7
    Going back to end my life,
     Am   E7   Am
Beneath the Rising Sun.

I Love To Tell The Story

Words by Katherine Hankey
Music by William G. Fischer

Verse 1

    G   **C**   **G**
I love to tell the story, of unseen things above,
    D7   **Gsus4**   **G**   **D7**
Of Jesus and His glory,   of Jesus and His love.
                     G   **Em**   **B**
I love to tell the story, because I know 'tis true;
  C   **G**   **D7**   **G**
It satisfies my longings, as nothing else can do.

Refrain

  D7   **Gsus4**
I love to tell the story!
G   **C**   **G**
'Twill be my theme in glory,
               C
To tell the old, old story,
  G/D **D7**   **G**
Of Jesus and His love.

Verse 2

    G   **C**   **G**
I love to tell the story, more wonderful it seems,
    D7   **Gsus4**   **G**   **D7**
Than all the golden fancies, of all our golden dreams.
                     G   **Em**   **B**
I love to tell the story, it did so much for me;
  C   **G**   **D7**   **G**
And that is just the reason, I tell it now to thee.

Refrain

  D7   **Gsus4**
I love to tell the story!
G   **C**   **G**
'Twill be my theme in glory,
               C
To tell the old, old story,
  G/D **D7**   **G**
Of Jesus and His love.

Copyright © 2008 Amsco Publications, a Division of Music Sales Corporation.
All Rights Reserved. International Copyright Secured.

Verse 3

G
I love to tell the story;
    C   **G**
'Tis pleasant to repeat what seems,
D7   **Gsus4**
Each time I tell it,
    G   **D7**
More wonderfully sweet.
          G   **Em**   **B**
I love to tell the story, for some have never heard,
     C   **G**   **D7**   **G**
The message of salvation, from God's own holy Word.

Refrain

    D7   **Gsus4**
I love to tell the story!
G   **C**   **G**
'Twill be my theme in glory,
           C
To tell the old, old story,
  G/D **D7**   **G**
Of Jesus and His love.

Verse 4

G   **C**   **G**
I love to tell the story, for those who know it best,
   D7   **Gsus4**   **G**   **D7**
Seem hungering and thirsting, to hear it like the rest.
           G   **Em**   **B**
And when, in scenes of glory, I sing the new, new song,
  C   **G**   **D7**   **G**
'Twill be the old, old story, that I have loved so long.

Refrain

    D7   **Gsus4**
I love to tell the story!
G   **C**   **G**
'Twill be my theme in glory,
           C
To tell the old, old story,
  G/D **D7**   **G**
Of Jesus and His love.

I'm On My Way
To Freedom Land

Traditional

Verse 1

           G   **D7**
I'm on my way to Freedom land,
                      G
I'm on my way to Freedom land,
    G7/D **G7**   **C**
I'm on my way to Freedom land,
   Am **G/D**   **D7**   **G**
I'm on my way, great God, I'm on my way.

Verse 2

           G   **D7**
I asked my brother to come with me,
                      G
I asked my brother to come with me,
    G7/D   **G7**   **C**
I asked my brother to come with me,
   Am **G/D**   **D7**   **G**
I'm on my way, great God, I'm on my way.

Verse 3

           G   **D7**
I asked my sister to come with me,
                      G
I asked my sister to come with me,
    G7/D   **G7**   **C**
I asked my sister to come with me,
   Am **G/D**   **D7**   **G**
I'm on my way, great God, I'm on my way.

Verse 4

           G   **D7**
I asked my boss to let me go,
                      G
I asked my boss to let me go,
    G7/D **G7**   **C**
I asked my boss to let me go,
   Am **G/D**   **D7**   **G**
I'm on my way, great God, I'm on my way.

Copyright © 2008 Amsco Publications, a Division of Music Sales Corporation.
All Rights Reserved. International Copyright Secured.

Verse 5

       G   **D7**
If he says no, I'll go anyhow,
                 G
If he says no, I'll go anyhow,
       G7/D G7   **C**
If he says no, I'll go anyhow,
   Am G/D   **D7**   **G**
I'm on my way, great God, I'm on my way.

Verse 6

           G   **D7**
If you won't go, let your children go,
                    G
If you won't go, let your children go,
       G7/D   **G7**   **C**
If you won't go, let your children go,
   Am G/D   **D7**   **G**
I'm on my way, great God, I'm on my way.

Verse 7

          G   **D7**
If you won't go, let your mother go,
                  G
If you won't go, let your mother go,
       G7/D   **G7**   **C**
If you won't go, let your mother go,
   Am G/D   **D7**   **G**
I'm on my way, great God, I'm on my way.

Verse 8

         G   **D7**
I'm on my way, and I won't turn back,
                   G
I'm on my way, and I won't turn back,
       G7/D   **G7**   **C**
I'm on my way, and I won't turn back,
   Am G/D   **D7**   **G**
I'm on my way, great God, I'm on my way.

In The Sweet By And By

Words by S. Fillmore Bennet
Music by J.P. Webster

Verse 1

$\quad\quad\quad\quad\quad$ **G** $\quad\quad\quad\quad$ **C** $\quad\quad\quad$ **G** $\quad$ **D7**
There's a land that is fairer than day,__
G $\quad\quad\quad\quad$ **G7** $\quad$ **E7** $\quad\quad$ **Am D7**
And by faith we can see it afar,___
$\quad\quad\quad\quad$ **G** $\quad\quad\quad\quad$ **C** $\quad\quad\quad$ **G** $\quad$ **D7**
For the Father waits over the way,__
G $\quad\quad\quad\quad\quad$ **D7** $\quad\quad\quad\quad$ **G**
To prepare us a dwelling place there.

Refrain

$\quad\quad\quad\quad\quad\quad\quad$ **Am**
In the sweet by and by,
$\quad\quad$ **D7** $\quad\quad\quad\quad\quad\quad\quad\quad$ **G**
We shall meet on that beautiful shore;
$\quad\quad$ **G7** $\quad\quad$ **C**
In the sweet by and by,
$\quad\quad$ **C♯° G** $\quad\quad\quad$ **Am D7 G**
We shall meet on that beautiful shore.

Verse 2

$\quad\quad\quad\quad$ **G** $\quad\quad\quad\quad$ **C** $\quad\quad\quad$ **G** $\quad\quad$ **D7**
We shall sing on that beautiful shore,__
G $\quad\quad\quad$ **G7** $\quad$ **E7** $\quad\quad\quad$ **Am** $\quad\quad$ **D7**
The melodious songs of the blessed;__
$\quad\quad\quad\quad$ **G** $\quad\quad\quad\quad$ **C** $\quad\quad\quad$ **G** $\quad$ **D7**
And our spirits shall sorrow no more,__
G $\quad\quad\quad\quad\quad$ **D7** $\quad\quad\quad$ **G**
Not a sigh for the blessing of rest.

Refrain

$\quad\quad\quad\quad\quad\quad\quad$ **Am**
In the sweet by and by,
$\quad\quad$ **D7** $\quad\quad\quad\quad\quad\quad\quad\quad$ **G**
We shall meet on that beautiful shore;
$\quad\quad$ **G7** $\quad\quad$ **C**
In the sweet by and by,
$\quad\quad$ **C♯° G** $\quad\quad\quad$ **Am D7 G**
We shall meet on that beautiful shore.

Copyright © 2008 Amsco Publications, a Division of Music Sales Corporation.
All Rights Reserved. International Copyright Secured.

		G	C	G	D7
Verse 3	To our bountiful Father above,__

        G   **C**   **G** **D7**

Verse 3   To our bountiful Father above,__

        G   **G7**   **E7**   **Am** **D7**

      We will offer our tribute of praise,__

        G   **C**   **G** **D7**

      For the glorious gift of His love,__

        G   **D7**   **G**

      And the blessings that hallow our days.

                    Am

Refrain   In the sweet by and by,

            D7   **G**

      We shall meet on that beautiful shore;

           G7   **C**

      In the sweet by and by,

        C#° **G**   **Am** **D7** **G**

      We shall meet on that beautiful shore.

I've Been Working
On The Railroad

Traditional

Verse 1

G
I've been working on the railroad,
C   **Cm G**
All the livelong day,

I've been working on the railroad,
      A7   **D7**
Just to pass the time away.
               D7
Can't you hear the whistle blowing,
C   **B7**
Rise up so early in the morn,
C   **C♯°7**   **G**
Don't you hear the captain shouting,
    D7   **G**
Dinah, blow your horn.

Refrain

Dinah, won't you blow,
A7
Dinah, won't you blow,
D7   **G**   **D7 G**
Dinah, won't you blow your horn?_____

Dinah, won't you blow,
A7
Dinah, won't you blow,
D7   **G**
Dinah, won't you blow your horn?

Copyright © 2008 Amsco Publications, a Division of Music Sales Corporation
International Copyright Secured. All Rights Reserved.

Verse 2

G
Someone's in the kitchen with Dinah,
                 D7
Someone's in the kitchen I know,
G   **G7 C C♯°7**
Someone's in the kitchen with Dinah,
G   **D7**   **G**
Strumming on the old banjo, and singing,

Fie-fi, fiddlee-i-o,
              D7
Fie-fi, fiddlee-i-o,
G G7 C   **C♯°7**
Fie-fi, fiddlee-i-o,
G/D   **D7**   **G**
Strumming on the old banjo.

Jesus Loves Me, This I Know

Words by Anna B. Warner
Music by William B. Bradbury

Verse 1

C   G7   C
Jesus loves me, this I know,
F   C
For the Bible tells me so.
     G7   C
Little ones to Him belong;
F   C   G7 C
They are weak, but He is strong.

Refrain

         F/C
Yes, Jesus loves me!
C   G7
Yes, Jesus loves me!
C   F/C
Yes, Jesus loves me!
    C   G7   C
The Bible tells me so.

Verse 2

C   G7   C
Jesus loves me, this I know,
F   C
As He loved so long ago,
     G7   C
Taking children on His knee,
F   C   G7   C
Saying, "Let them come to Me."

Refrain

         F/C
Yes, Jesus loves me!
C   G7
Yes, Jesus loves me!
C   F/C
Yes, Jesus loves me!
    C   G7   C
The Bible tells me so.

Copyright © 2008 Amsco Publications, a Division of Music Sales Corporation.
All Rights Reserved. International Copyright Secured.

Verse 3

  C **G7** **C**
Jesus loves me, He will stay,
F   **C**
Close beside me all the way;
 G7 **C**
If I love him when I die,
F **C** **G7** **C**
He will take me home on high.

Refrain

     F/C
Yes, Jesus loves me!
C   **G7**
Yes, Jesus loves me!
C   **F/C**
Yes, Jesus loves me!
  C **G7** **C**
The Bible tells me so.

Verse 4

C **G7** **C**
Jesus take this heart of mine,
F   **C**
Make it pure and wholly Thine,
   G7 **C**
Thou has bled and died for me,
F **C**   **G7** **C**
I will henceforth live for Thee.

Refrain

     F/C
Yes, Jesus loves me!
C   **G7**
Yes, Jesus loves me!
C   **F/C**
Yes, Jesus loves me!
  C **G7** **C**
The Bible tells me so.

Jesus, Savior, Pilot Me

Words by Edward Hopper
Music by John E. Gould

Verse 1

      G   **C** **G**
Jesus, Savior, pilot me,
D7 **Cmaj7** **G/D** **D7** **G**
Over life's tempes - tuous sea;
       D7   **G**
Unknown waves before me roll,
    D7   **G**
Hiding rock and treacherous shoal.
          C   **G**
Chart and compass came from Thee;
D7 **Cmaj7** **G/D** **D7** **G**
Jesus, Savior, pi - lot me.

Verse 2

      G   **C**   **G**
While th' Apostles' fragile bark,
D7   **Cmaj7** **G/D** **D7** **G**
Struggled with the bil - lows dark,
    D7   **G**
On the stormy Galilee,
     D7   **G**
Thou didst walk upon the sea;
         C   **G**
And when they beheld Thy form,
D7   **Cmaj7** **G/D**   **D7** **G**
Safe they glided through the storm.

Verse 3

      G   **C**   **G**
Though the sea be smooth and bright,
D7   **Cmaj7** **G/D** **D7** **G**
Sparkling with the stars of night,
     D7   **G**
And my ship's path be ablaze,
     D7   **G**
With the light of halcyon days,
       C   **G**
Still I know my need of Thee;
D7 **Cmaj7** **G/D** **D7** **G**
Jesus, Savior, pi - lot me.

Copyright © 2008 Amsco Publications, a Division of Music Sales Corporation.
All Rights Reserved. International Copyright Secured.

Verse 4

<pre>
        G   C   G
When the darkling heavens frown,
D7   Cmaj7 G/D   D7   G
And the wrathful winds come down,
                D7   G
And the fierce waves, tossed on high,
                D7   G
Lash themselves against the sky,
            C   G
Jesus, Savior, pilot me,
D7   Cmaj7 G/D D7   G
Over life's tempes - tuous sea.
</pre>

Verse 5

<pre>
        G   C   G
As a mother stills her child,
D7   Cmaj7 G/D D7 G
Thou canst hush the o -   cean wild,
                D7   G
Boisterous waves obey Thy will,
                D7   G
When Thou sayest to them, "Be still!"
                C   G
Wondrous Sovereign of the sea,
D7   Cmaj7 G/D D7 G
Jesus, Savior, pi - lot me.
</pre>

Verse 6

<pre>
        G C   G
When at last I near the shore,
D7   Cmaj7 G/D D7 G
And the fearful   brea - kers roar,
                D7   G
'Twixt me and the peaceful rest,
                D7   G
Then, while leaning on Thy breast,
            C   G
May I hear Thee say to me,
D7   Cmaj7 G/D D7   G
"Fear not, I will pi - lot thee."
</pre>

I Want To Be In Dixie

Words and Music by Irving Berlin

<pre>
        A   E7   A
I want to be, I want to be,
   E7   A   C#7   D
I want to be down home in Dixie,
F#m7   B7
Where the hens are doggone glad to lay,
                        E7
Scrambled eggs in the new mown hay,
            A   E7   A
You ought to see, you ought to see,
   E7   A   C#7   D
You ought to see my home in Dixie,
F7b5   A   A+   D Dm A
You can tell the world I'm going   to,
   E7 A   Bm7 A
D-I-X, I don't know how to spell it but I'm goin',
   E7   A   F7b5 A   F#m Bm7 E7 A
You bet I'm goin' to my home in   Dix - ie   land.
</pre>

Copyright © 2008 Amsco Publications, a Division of Music Sales Corporation.
All Rights Reserved. International Copyright Secured.

Jingle Bells

Words an Music by J.S. Pierpont

Verse 1

G
Dashing through the snow,
          C
In a one horse open sleigh,
Am   **D7**
O'er the fields we go,
          G
Laughing all the way,

Bells on bob tails ring,
         C
Making spirits bright,
      Am   **G**
What fun it is to ride and sing,
          G
A sleighing song tonight.

Refrain

D7 G
Oh, jingle bells, jingle bells,
      Am **G**
Jingle all the way.
C   **G**
Oh, what fun it is to ride,
    A7   **D7**
In a one horse open sleigh.
      G
Hey! Jingle bells, jingle bells,
      Am **G**
Jingle all the way.
C   **G**
Oh, what fun it is to ride,
    D7   **G**
In a one horse open sleigh.

Copyright © 2008 Amsco Publications, a Division of Music Sales Corporation.
All Rights Reserved. International Copyright Secured.

Verse 2

G
A day or two ago,
            C
I thought I'd take a ride,
   Am   D7
And soon Miss Fanny Bright,
       G
Was seated by my side,

The horse was lean and lank,
           C
Misfortune seemed his lot,
   Am   G
We got into a drifted bank,
         G
And then we got upsot.

Refrain

D7 G
Oh, jingle bells, jingle bells,
    Am G
Jingle all the way.
C   G
Oh, what fun it is to ride,
  A7   D7
In a one horse open sleigh.
     G
Hey! Jingle bells, jingle bells,
    Am G
Jingle all the way.
C   G
Oh, what fun it is to ride,
  D7   G
In a one horse open sleigh.

Verse 3
Now the ground is white,
C
Go it while you're young,
Am   **D7**
Take the girls tonight,
G
And sing this sleighing song.

Just get a bob-tailed nag,
C
Two-forty for his speed,
Am   **G**
Then hitch him to an open sleigh,
G
And crack! you'll take the lead!

D7 G

Refrain
Oh, jingle bells, jingle bells,
Am **G**
Jingle all the way.
C   **G**
Oh, what fun it is to ride,
A7   **D7**
In a one horse open sleigh.
G
Hey! Jingle bells, jingle bells,
Am **G**
Jingle all the way.
C   **G**
Oh, what fun it is to ride,
D7   **G**
In a one horse open sleigh.

Joy To The World

Words by Isaac Watts
Traditional

Verse 1

   D   **Em D**   **A D**
Joy to the world! The Lord is come;
  G   **A7**   **D**
Let earth receive her King.

Let ev'ry heart prepare Him room,

And heaven and nature sing,
    A
And heaven and nature sing,
     D   **G**   **D**   **Em D**   **A7**
And heaven, and heaven, and nature sing.

Verse 2

   D   **Em D** **A D**
Joy to the world! The Savior reigns;
  G   **A7**   **D**
Let men their songs employ,

While fields and floods, rocks, hills and plains,

Repeat the sounding joy,
    A
Repeat the sounding joy,
    D   **G**   **D** **Em** **D** **A7**
Repeat, repeat, the sounding joy.

Verse 3

   D   **Em D A**   **D**
No more let sins and sorrows grow,
  G   **A7**   **D**
Nor thorns infest the ground,

He comes to make His blessings flow,

Far as the curse is found,
    A
Far as the curse is found,
    D   **G** **D** **Em** **D** **A7**
Far as, far as, the curse is found.

Copyright © 2008 Amsco Publications, a Division of Music Sales Corporation.
All Rights Reserved. International Copyright Secured.

Verse 2

        G   **C/G** **G**
Overseas there came a pleading,
            C Cm G
"Help a nation in dis - tress."
      D   **D7**   **G**
And we gave our glorious laddies,
Em   **D**   **A7** **D**
Honor bade us do no less,
      G   **C/G** **G**
For no gallant son of freedom,
       C   **Cm** **G**
To a tyrant's yoke should bend,
    Bm   **Em7**
And a noble heart must answer,
     D/A **Em7 A7 D**
To the sacred call of "Friend."

Refrain

G   **G/D** **D7**
Keep the home fires burn - ing,
Em   **B+** **B7**
While your hearts are yearning,
C   **G**
Though your lads are far away,
    A7   **D7**
They dream of home.
G   **G/D** **D7**
There's a silver lin - ing,
Em   **B+** **B7**
Through the dark clouds shin - ing,
C   **G**
Turn the dark cloud inside out,
C   **G/D** **D7** **G**
'Til the boys come home.

Kentucky Babe

Words by Richard H. Buck
Music by Adam Geibel

Verse 1

C
Skeeters am a hummin', on the honeysuckle vine,
       G7
Sleep, Kentucky babe.

Sandman am a comin', to this little babe of mine,
D7   **G**
Sleep, Kentucky babe.
C
Silv'ry moon am a shinin' in the heavens up above,

Bobolink am pinin' for his little lady love.
       G7   **Fm7** **G7**   **Fm7**
You is mighty lucky, babe of old Kentucky,
G   **D7**   **G7**
Close your eyes in sleep.

Refrain

C
Fly away, fly away Kentucky babe,

Fly away to rest.
G7
Fly away,
Dm7   **G7**
Lay your little sleepy head,
C
On your mammy's breast,
A♭ **C** **A♭** **C**
Hm,__ Hm, _
      G7 **C** **G7** **C**
Close your eyes and sleep.

Copyright © 2008 Amsco Publications, a Division of Music Sales Corporation.
All Rights Reserved. International Copyright Secured.

Verse 2

C
Daddy's in the canebrake with his little dog and gun,
         G7
Sleep, Kentucky babe.

'Possum for your breakfast when your sleepin' time is done,
D7   **G**
Sleep, Kentucky babe.
C
Bogey man'll catch you sure unless you close your eyes,

Waitin' just outside your door to take you by surprise.
      G7   **Fm7 G7**   **Fm7**
Best be keepin' shady, pretty little lady,

Close your eyes and sleep.

Refrain

C
Fly away, fly away Kentucky babe,

Fly away to rest.
G7
Fly away,
Dm7   **G7**
Lay your little sleepy head,
C
On your mammy's breast,
A♭ C A♭ C
Hm,__ Hm, _
    G7 C G7 C
Close your eyes and sleep.

Let My People Go

Traditional

Verse 1

       Gm D   **Gm**
When Israel was in Egypt's land,
D7
Let my people go.
              D   **Gm**
Oppressed so hard they could not stand,
D7   **Gm**
Let my people go.

Refrain

       Cm
Go down, Moses,
D
Way down in Egypt's land,
Gm
Tell old Pharaoh,
D7   **Gm**
Let my people go.

Verse 2

       Gm D   **Gm**
No more shall they in bondage toil,
D7
Let my people go.
              D   **Gm**
Let them come out with Egypt's spoil,
D7   **Gm**
Let my people go.

Refrain

       Cm
Go down, Moses,
D
Way down in Egypt's land,
Gm
Tell old Pharaoh,
D7   **Gm**
Let my people go.

Copyright © 2008 Amsco Publications, a Division of Music Sales Corporation.
All Rights Reserved. International Copyright Secured.

Verse 3

      Gm **D**   **Gm**
Oh, let us all from bondage flee,
D7
Let my people go.
     D   **Gm**
And let us all in Christ be free,
D7   **Gm**
Let my people go.

Refrain

        Cm
Go down, Moses,
D
Way down in Egypt's land,
Gm
Tell old Pharaoh,
D7   **Gm**
Let my people go.

Verse 4

      Gm   **D**   **Gm**
You need not always weep and mourn,
D7
Let my people go.
     D   **Gm**
And wear these slav'ry chains forlorn,
D7   **Gm**
Let my people go.

Refrain

        Cm
Go down, Moses,
D
Way down in Egypt's land,
Gm
Tell old Pharaoh,
D7   **Gm**
Let my people go.

Verse 5

            Gm   **D**   **Gm**
Your foes shall not before you stand,
D7
Let my people go.
          D   **Gm**
And you'll possess fair Canaan's land,
D7   **Gm**
Let my people go.

Refrain

              Cm
Go down, Moses,
D
Way down in Egypt's land,
Gm
Tell old Pharaoh,
D7   **Gm**
Let my people go.

Listen To The Mockingbird

Words by Alice Hawthorne
Music by Richard Milburn

Verse 1

$\quad\quad$ G $\quad\quad$ D7 $\quad$ G
I'm dreaming now of Hallie,
$\quad\quad$ D7 $\quad\quad\quad$ G
Sweet Hallie, sweet Hallie,
$\quad\quad$ D7 $\quad\quad\quad\quad$ G
I'm dreaming now of Hallie,
$\quad\quad\quad\quad$ C $\quad\quad\quad\quad\quad$ D7 $\quad\quad\quad$ G
For the thought of her is one that never dies.
$\quad\quad\quad\quad$ D7 $\quad$ G
She's sleeping in the valley,
$\quad\quad$ D7 $\quad\quad\quad\quad$ G
The valley, in the valley,
$\quad\quad$ D7 $\quad\quad\quad$ G
She's sleeping in the valley,
$\quad\quad\quad$ C $\quad\quad\quad\quad\quad$ D7 $\quad\quad\quad\quad$ G
And the mockingbird is singing where she lies.

Refrain

$\quad\quad\quad\quad$ D7 $\quad\quad\quad\quad\quad\quad\quad\quad\quad\quad$ G
Listen to the mockingbird, listen to the mockingbird,
$\quad\quad$ D7 $\quad\quad\quad\quad\quad\quad\quad\quad\quad$ G
The mockingbird still singing o'er her grave.
$\quad\quad\quad\quad$ D7 $\quad\quad\quad\quad\quad\quad\quad\quad\quad$ G
Listen to the mockingbird, listen to the mockingbird,
G7 $\quad\quad\quad\quad\quad\quad\quad\quad$ D7 $\quad\quad\quad$ G
Still singing where the weeping willows wave.

Copyright © 2008 Amsco Publications, a Division of Music Sales Corporation.
All Rights Reserved. International Copyright Secured.

Verse 2

       G   **D7** **G**
Ah! well I yet remember,
 D7   **G**
Remember, remember,
   D7   **G**
Ah! well, I yet remember,
        C   **D7**   **G**
When we gathered in the cotton side by side.
         D7   **G**
'Twas in the mild September,
  D7   **G**
September, September,
    D7   **G**
'Twas in the mild September,
    C   **D7**   **G**
And the mockingbird is singing far and wide.

Refrain

          D7   **G**
Listen to the mockingbird, listen to the mockingbird,
 D7   **G**
The mockingbird still singing o'er her grave.
         D7   **G**
Listen to the mockingbird, listen to the mockingbird,
G7   **D7**   **G**
Still singing where the weeping willows wave.

Verse 3

        G   **D7**   **G**
When charms of spring are awaken,
    D7   **G**
Are awaken, are awaken,
    D7   **G**
When charms of spring are awaken,
      C   **D7**   **G**
And the mockingbird is singing on the bough.
          D7 G
I feel like one so for - saken,
    D7   **G**
So forsaken, so forsaken,
  D7   **G**
I feel like one so forsaken,
      C   **D7**   **G**
Since my Hallie is no longer with me now.

Refrain

        D7   **G**
Listen to the mockingbird, listen to the mockingbird,
    D7   **G**
The mockingbird still singing o'er her grave.
        D7   **G**
Listen to the mockingbird, listen to the mockingbird,
G7   **D7**   **G**
Still singing where the weeping willows wave.

Let Us Break Bread Together

Traditional

Intro | F   Dm | Gm7   C7 |

| F   B♭ | F |

Verse 1

      F   Dm   Gm7 C7   F   B♭
Let us break bread together on our knees,___
F   Am   F   Dm7 G7   C   F
  Let us break bread together on our knees._
C   F   Cm   D7
  When I fall on my knees,
      Gm   Gm7 C7
With my face to the rising sun,
    F   F7   Dm   Gm C7 F   B♭6 F
Oh Lord, have mercy on ___ me._____

Verse 2

      F   Dm   Gm7 C7   F   B♭
Let us drink wine together on our knees,___
F   Am   F   Dm7 G7   C   F
  Let us drink wine together on our knees.__
C   F   Cm   D7
  When I fall on my knees,
      Gm   Gm7 C7
With my face to the rising sun,
    F   F7   Dm   Gm C7 F   B♭6 F
Oh Lord, have mercy on ___ me._____

Interlude | F   Dm | Gm7   C7 |

| F   B♭ | F |

Copyright © 2008 Amsco Publications, a Division of Music Sales Corporation.
All Rights Reserved. International Copyright Secured.

Verse 3

      F   **Dm**   **Gm7 C7**   **F**   **B♭**
Let us praise God together on our knees,___
F   **Am** **F**   **Dm7** **G7**   **C**   **F**
  Let us praise God together on our knees.__
C   **F**   **Cm**   **D7**
  When I fall on my knees,
      Gm   **Gm7 C7**
With my face to the rising sun,
    F   **F7**   **Dm**   **Gm C7 F** **B♭6** **F**
Oh Lord, have mercy on ___ me._____

Little Brown Jug

Words and Music by Joseph E. Winner

Verse 1

      C   F/A Dm
My wife and I live all   alone,
    G7   C
In a little log hut we call our own,
                    F/A Dm
She loves gin and I love rum,
    G7   C   G7 C
I tell you we had lots of   fun.

Refrain

             F
Ha, ha, ha, you and me,
G7   C G7 C
Little brown jug, how I   love thee,
             F
Ha, ha, ha, you and me,
G7   C G7 C
Little brown jug, how I   love thee.

Verse 2

      C   F/A   Dm
'Tis you who makes my friends and foes,
    G7   C
'Tis you that makes me wear old clothes,
                   F/A   Dm
Here you are you are so near my nose,
    G7   C   G7 C
So tip her up and down she goes.

Refrain

             F
Ha, ha, ha, you and me,
G7   C G7 C
Little brown jug, how I   love thee,
             F
Ha, ha, ha, you and me,
G7   C G7 C
Little brown jug, how I   love thee.

Copyright © 2008 Amsco Publications, a Division of Music Sales Corporation.
All Rights Reserved. International Copyright Secured.

Verse 3

```
        C              F/A   Dm
When I go toiling on the farm,
G7      C
Little jug under my arm,
                  F/A   Dm
Place him under a shady tree,
G7              C G7   C
Little brown, don't I   love thee?
```

Refrain

```
              F
Ha, ha, ha, you and me,
G7              C  G7  C
Little brown jug, how I   love thee,
              F
Ha, ha, ha, you and me,
G7              C  G7  C
Little brown jug, how I   love thee.
```

Verse 4

```
C                      F/A   Dm
Crossed the creek on a hollow log,
G7              C
Me and the wife and the little brown dog,
                  F/A   Dm
The wife and the dog fell in, kerplunk,
  G7          C   G7   C
But I held on to the little brown jug.
```

Refrain

```
              F
Ha, ha, ha, you and me,
G7              C  G7  C
Little brown jug, how I   love thee,
              F
Ha, ha, ha, you and me,
G7              C  G7  C
Little brown jug, how I   love thee.
```

Verse 5

                C   F/A   Dm
One day when I went out to my barn,
G7   C
Little brown jug under my arm,
                        F/A   Dm
Tripped my toe and down I fell,
G7   C   G7 C
Broke that little jug to   hell.

Refrain

                    F
Ha, ha, ha, you and me,
G7   C G7 C
Little brown jug, how I   love thee,
                    F
Ha, ha, ha, you and me,
G7   C G7 C
Little brown jug, how I   love thee.

Meet Me In St. Louis, Louis

Words by Andrew B. Sterline
Music by Kerry Mill

C
Meet me in St. Louis, Louis,
F
Meet me at the fair,

Don't tell me the lights are shining
D7   **G7**
Any place but there;
      E7   **A7**
We will dance the Hoochee Koochee,
      D7   **G7**
I will be your tootsie wootsie,
      C
If you will meet in St. Louis, Louis,
D7   **G7**   **C**
Meet me at the fair.

Copyright © 2008 Amsco Publications, a Division of Music Sales Corporation.
All Rights Reserved. International Copyright Secured.

The Marines' Hymn

Traditional

Verse 1

B9sus4 E   B7/A E/G♯ B7/F♯ E
From the Halls of   Mon - tezu - ma,
F°7   B9sus4 B7   E
To the shores of Tripoli,
B9sus4 E   B7/A B7/F♯   E
We   fight our   country's battles,
F°7   B9sus4 B7   E F♯m7
On the land as   on the sea.____
E/G♯   A   E
     First to fight for right and freedom,
          A   E   F°7 B7/F♯
And to keep our honor clean,_____
B9sus4 E   B7/A E/G♯ B7/F♯ E
We are   proud to   claim the   title,
Amaj7 F♯m7♭5 E/B Fm   B7 E
Of   U   -   nited States Marines.

Verse 2

B9sus4 E   B7/A   E/G♯ B7/F♯ E
Our   flag's unfurled to eve - ry   breeze,
F°7 B9sus4 B7   E
From dawn to setting sun,
B9sus4 E   B7/A B7/F♯   E
We have fought in every clime and place,
F°7   B9sus4 B7 E F♯m7
Where we could take a gun.
E/G♯   A   E
     In the snow of far-off Northern lands,
       A   E   F°7 B7/F♯
And in sunny tropic scenes,_____
B9sus4 E   B7/A E/G♯ B7/F♯ E
You will find us always on   the   job,
Amaj7 F♯m7♭5 E/B   Fm   B7 E
The   U   -   nited States Marines.

Copyright © 2008 Amsco Publications, a Division of Music Sales Corporation.
All Rights Reserved. International Copyright Secured.

B9sus4 E   B7/A E/G♯ B7/F♯ E
Here's   health to   you and to our Corps,
F°7   B9sus4 B7   E
Which we are   proud to serve,
B9sus4 E   B7/A B7/F♯   E
In many a strife we've fought for life,
F°7 B9sus4 B7   E   F♯m7
And never   lost our nerve.____
E/G♯   A   E
      If the Army and the Navy,
      A   E   F°7 B7/F♯
Ever look on Heaven's scenes,_____
B9sus4 E   B7/A E/G♯ B7/F♯ E
They will find the   streets are   guarded,
Amaj7 F♯m7♭5 E/B Fm B7 E
By   U   -   nited States Marines.

Memorial Day

Words and Music by Susanna Blamire

Verse 1

```
      E  B  E      B        E/B  B7
Today the earth is dressed in      green,
         E           A/E      E/B  B
And decked with sweetest flow - ers,
E           A/E E      A  E
And all the sky  smiles overhead,
A6 E/B            B7 E
To  bless this land of  ours.
                C#m     E
No bloody fields portray today,
A/E  E   A/E  E            E/B  B
The   country's priceless cost,___
E                A/E  E  C#m B7  E
Scarce lovelier could the  world have looked,
A  E    A  E/B B7 E
Ere par - a - dise   was lost.
```

Verse 2

```
      E   B  E      B      E/B  B7
Above the fields of former   strife,
         E        A/E    E/B  B
Now starts the waving grain,___
E          A/E E       A        E
And all is bloom and light and life,
A6    E/B          B7 E
Where heroes brave were slain.
                C#m      E
Bring sweetest flow'rs to deck the graves,
A/E  E    A/E  E  E/B B
Where noble forms are laid,___
E          A/E  E  C#m B7  E
Bring amaranths and ev  -  er - greens,
A  E    A  E/B B7 E
Not those that ear - ly   fade.
```

Copyright © 2008 Amsco Publications, a Division of Music Sales Corporation.
All Rights Reserved. International Copyright Secured.

Verse 3

```
                E  B  E      B  E/B  B7
```
Plant myrtle and forget-me-nots,
```
          E     A/E  E/B  B
```
And roses white and   red;
```
E            A/E     E      A  E
```
Twine laurel wreaths around the stones,
```
A6    E/B      B7        E
```
Where sleep our martyred dead.
```
             C♯m     E
```
And in the heart and on the lip,
```
A/E  E    A/E E   E/B  B
```
Let   those who lie away,___
```
E          A/E    E   C♯m  B7 E
```
Far off in swamps and in   the sea,
```
A   E     A  E/B B7  E
```
Be crowned   with bay.

The Memphis Blues

Words by George A. Norton
Music by W.C. Handy

Intro | **C7**　　　　| **F**　**C7**　|

　　　　　| **F**　　　　　|　　　　　|

Verse 1

‖: You want to be my man,
　　　　　F7　　　　　　　　　**B♭**　**B♭m F**
You gotta give me forty dollars down.
B°7　　　　　**B♭7**
　　You want to be my man,
　　　　　　　　　　　　F
You'll give me forty dollars down.
　　　　　C7/G　　**C7**
If you don't be my man,___
　　　F/C　　　　　**C7**　　　**F**
Your baby's gonna shake this town. :‖

Refrain

F♯°　**C7/G**
Mister Crump don't 'low,
　　　　　　　　F
No easy riders here.
C7/G
Crump don't 'low,
　　　　　　A
No easy riders here.
A7 D7
　　We don't care what Mister Crump don't 'low,
Gm
We gonna bar'l house any how,
　　　　　C7/G
Mister Crump don't 'low,
　　　　　F
No easy riders here.

Interlude | **C7**　　　　| **F**　**C7**　|

　　　　　　| **F**　　　　　|　　　　　|

Copyright © 2008 Amsco Publications, a Division of Music Sales Corporation.
All Rights Reserved. International Copyright Secured.

Verse 2

$B\flat$

‖: I'm goin' down the river,

Goin' down the river,

$B\flat7$

Gonna to take my rockin' chair.

$E\flat$

Goin' in the river,

$G°$ $E\flat$ $B\flat$

Gonna to take my rockin' chair.

$F7$

Blues overtake me,

$B\flat/F$ $F7$ $B\flat$ $F7$

Gonna rock away from here.

$B\flat$

Oh, the Mississippi River,

$B\flat7$

Mississippi River, so deep and wide,___

$E\flat$ $B\flat$

I said, the Mississippi River's so deep and wide,

$F7$ $B\flat$

Man I love, he is on the other side. :‖

A Mighty Fortress Is Our God

Words and Music by Martin Luther

Verse 1

C   G   Am D7 G
A mighty fortress is   our God,
A Em F   C A Dm G7 C
A bul - wark never fail - ing;
            G   Am D7 G
Our helper He, amid the flood
Am Em F C A Dm G7 C
Of   mor - tal ills prevail -   ing:
         Am G C D7 G
For still our an - cient foe,
C   G   C F   E Am
Doth seek to work us woe;
E Am G Am   D7 G
His craft and power are great,
Dm F   C   A Dm E
And, armed with cruel   hate,
Am Dm6 C A Dm G7 C
On   earth is not his e   -   qual.

Verse 2

C   G   Am   D7 G
Did we in our own strength confide,
A Em F C   A Dm G7 C
Our striving would be los - ing;
            G   Am D7 G
Were not the right Man on our side,
Am Em F C   A   Dm G7 C
The Man of God's own choos - ing:
         Am G C D7 G
Dost ask who that   may be
C   G C F E Am
Christ Jesus, it is He;
E   Am G Am D7 G
Lord Sabaoth, is   His Name,
Dm F   C A Dm E
From age to age the   same,
Am Dm6 C A Dm G7 C
And He must win the bat - tle.

Copyright © 2008 Amsco Publications, a Division of Music Sales Corporation.
All Rights Reserved. International Copyright Secured.

Verse 3

```
C                    G      Am D7   G
And though this world, with devils filled,
A      Em  F   C  A Dm G7 C
Should threaten to undo_____ us,
              G       Am  D7  G
We will not fear, for God hath willed,
Am Em  F C A    Dm     G7 C
His  truth to triumph through___ us:
      Am   G   C   D7   G
The Prince of  Darkness grim,
C   G   C   F   E  Am
We tremble not for him;
E  Am  G  Am  D7 G
His rage we can en - dure,
Dm  F   C  A     Dm E
For  lo, his doom is   sure,
Am Dm6  C     A    Dm G7   C
One little   word shall fell____ him.
```

Verse 4

```
C             G        Am D7 G
That word above all earthly   powers,
A  Em   F   C    A  Dm G7  C
No thanks to  them, a - bid  -   eth;
              G       Am  D7  G
The Spirit and the gifts are  ours,
Am     Em  F   C    A Dm G7 C
Through Him, Who with us sid   -   eth:
      Am   G   C   D7   G
Let goods and kindred go,
C   G   C   F   E  Am
This mortal life al - so;
E   Am   G  Am  D7 G
The bo  - dy they  may kill:
Dm  F     C  A   Dm E
God's truth a - bideth  still,
Am Dm6  C     A  Dm G7  C
His  king - dom is  for - ev - er.
```

My Bonnie Lies Over The Ocean

Traditional

Verse 1

    A   D   A
My Bonnie lies over the ocean,
                    E7 Bm7 E7
My Bonnie lies over the sea,_____
    A   D   A
My Bonnie lies over the ocean,
   D   E   A
Oh bring back my Bonnie to me.

Refrain

            D
Bring back, bring back,
E7   A
Bring back my Bonnie to me, to me.
            D   B
Bring back, bring back,
E7   A
Bring back my Bonnie to me.

Verse 2

    A   D   A
Last night as I lay on my pillow,
                 E7 Bm7 E7
Last night as I lay on my bed.
    A   D   A
Last night as I lay on my pillow,
   D   E   A
I dreamed that my Bonnie was dead.

Refrain

            D
Bring back, bring back,
E7   A
Bring back my Bonnie to me, to me.
            D   B
Bring back, bring back,
E7   A
Bring back my Bonnie to me.

Copyright © 2008 Amsco Publications, a Division of Music Sales Corporation.
All Rights Reserved. International Copyright Secured.

Verse 3

     A   **D**   **A**
Oh blow ye the winds over the ocean,
                  E7 **Bm7 E7**
And blow ye the winds over the   sea.
     A   **D**   **A**
Oh blow ye the winds over the ocean,
     D   **E**   **A**
And bring back my Bonnie to me.

Refrain

          D
Bring back, bring back,
E7   **A**
Bring back my Bonnie to me, to me.
          D   **B**
Bring back, bring back,
E7   **A**
Bring back my Bonnie to me.

Verse 4

     A   **D**   **A**
The winds have blown over the ocean,
                  E7 **Bm7 E7**
The winds have blown over the   sea.
     A   **D**   **A**
The winds have blown over the ocean,
     E7   **A**
And brought back my Bonnie to me.

Refrain

          D
Bring back, bring back,
E7   **A**
Bring back my Bonnie to me, to me.
          D   **B**
Bring back, bring back,
E7   **A**
Bring back my Bonnie to me.

My Old Kentucky Home

Words and Music by Stephen Foster

Verse 1

     F   C7   F
Oh, the sun shines bright in the old Kentucky home,
    G7   C7
'Tis summer, the folks all are gay;
  F   C7   F
The corn-top's ripe and the meadow's in the bloom,
      C7   F
While the birds make music all the day;
           C7   F
The young folks roll on the little cabin floor,
    G7   C7
All merry, all happy, and bright,
  F   C7   F
By'n by hard times come a-knocking at the door,
       C7   F
Then my old Kentucky home, good night!

Refrain

    C7   F   C7 Dm B♭   F
Weep no more, my lady, oh weep no more today!
           C7   F
We will sing one song for the old Kentucky home,
    C7   F
For the old Kentucky home far away.

Verse 2

   F   C7   F
They hunt no more for the 'possum and the 'coon,
      G7   C7
On meadow, the hill and the shore,
   F   C7   F
They sing no more by the glimmer of the moon,
      C7   F
On the bench by that old cabin door;
      C7   F
The day goes by like a shadow o'er the heart,
    G7   C7
With sorrow where all was delight;
  F   C7   F
The time has come when the people have to part,
       C7   F
Then my old Kentucky home, good night!

Copyright © 2008 Amsco Publications, a Division of Music Sales Corporation.
All Rights Reserved. International Copyright Secured.

Refrain

       C7   **F**   **C7 Dm**   **B♭**   **F**
Weep no more, my lady, oh weep no more today!
                         C7   **F**
We will sing one song for the old Kentucky home,
              C7   **F**
For the old Kentucky home far away.

Verse 3

      F   **C7**   **F**
The head must bow and the back will have to bend,
          G7   **C7**
Wherever the people may go;
  F   **C7**   **F**
A few more days and the trouble all will end,
           C7   **F**
In the field where sugar-canes may grow;
              C7   **F**
A few more days for to tote the weary load,
        G7   **C7**
No matter, 'twill never be light,
  F   **C7**   **F**
A few more days till we totter on the road,
           C7   **F**
Then my old Kentucky home, good night!

Refrain

       C7   **F**   **C7 Dm**   **B♭**   **F**
Weep no more, my lady, oh weep no more today!
                         C7   **F**
We will sing one song for the old Kentucky home,
              C7   **F**
For the old Kentucky home far away.

The Navy Hymn

Words by William Whiting
Music by John B. Dykes

Intro | C   F   C | G7   C |

| F   C |

Verse 1

                F   **C**
Eternal Father, strong to save,
        D   **G**   **Dsus4 D** **G**
Whose arm doth bind the rest - less wave,
  G7   **C**   **A7**   **D**
Who bid'st the mighty ocean deep,
    Em   **C**   **B7**   **Em**
Its own appointed limits keep;
  C7   **F**   **D7**   **G**
O hear us when we cry to Thee,
    C   **F C** **G7**   **C**
For those in peril on the sea.

Interlude | C | G |

| C   F   C | G7   C |

Verse 2

                F   **C**
O savior whose almighty word,
       D **G**   **Dsus4 D** **G**
The winds and waves submis - sive heard,
  G7   **C**   **A7**   **D**
Who walked'st on the foaming deep,
    Em   **C**   **B7 Em**
And calm amidst its rage did sleep;
  C7   **F**   **D7**   **G**
O hear us when we cry to Thee,
    C   **F C** **G7**   **C**
For those in peril on the sea!

Copyright © 2008 Amsco Publications, a Division of Music Sales Corporation.
All Rights Reserved. International Copyright Secured.

| C | | | | G | |
| C | F | C | | G7 | C | |

Verse 3

                F   C
O sacred spirit, who did'st brood,
         D G Dsus4 D G
Upon the waters dark   and rude,
     G7   C   A7   D
And bid their angry tumult cease,
      Em   C   B7   Em
And give, for wild confusion, peace:
  C7   F   D7   G
O hear us when we cry to Thee,
     C   F C G7   C
For those in peril on the sea.

| C | | | G | |
| C | F | C | | G7 | C | |

Verse 4

                F   C
O Trinity of love and power!
          D   G Dsus4 D   G
Our brethren shield in dan - ger's hour;
     G7   C   A7   D
From rock and tempest, fire and foe,
      Em   C   B7   Em
Protect them wheresoe'er they go;
    C7 F   D7   G
Thus evermore shall rise to Thee,
     C   F C   G7   C
Glad hymns of praise from land and sea.

Nearer, My God, To Thee

Words by Sarah Flower Adams
Music by Lowell Mason

Verse 1

F   C7 Dm B♭
Nearer, my God, to Thee,
F   C
Nearer to Thee,
F   C7   Dm B♭
E'en though it   be a cross,
F/C C7   F
That raiseth me,
       B♭/F F
Still all   my songs shall be,
     B♭/F F   C
Nearer,   my God, to Thee.
F   B♭
Nearer, my God, to Thee,
F/C C7 F
Nearer to Thee.

Verse 2

F   C7 Dm B♭
Though like the wanderer,
F   C
The sun gone down,
F   C7 Dm B♭
Darkness be over me,
F/C C7   F
My   rest a stone.
     B♭/F F
Yet in   my dreams I'd be,
     B♭/F F   C
Nearer,   my God, to Thee.
F   B♭
Nearer, my God, to Thee,
F/C C7 F
Nearer to Thee.

Copyright © 2008 Amsco Publications, a Division of Music Sales Corporation.
All Rights Reserved. International Copyright Secured.

Verse 3

F   C7 Dm B♭
There let the way appear,
F   C
Steps unto Heav'n,
F C7 Dm   B♭
All that Thou sendest me,
F/C C7   F
In   mercy given,
   B♭/F F
Angels to beckon me,
   B♭/F F   C
Nearer,   my God, to Thee.
F   B♭
Nearer, my God, to Thee,
F/C C7   F
Nearer to Thee.

Verse 4

F   C7 Dm B♭
Then, with my waking thoughts,
F   C
Bright with Thy praise,
F   C7 Dm B♭
Out of   my   stony griefs,
F/C   C7 F
Bethel I'll raise,
   B♭/F F
So by   my woes to be,
   B♭/F F   C
Nearer,   my God, to Thee.
F   B♭
Nearer, my God, to Thee,
F/C C7   F
Nearer to Thee.

Verse 5

F   C7 Dm B♭
Or, if on   joyful wing,
F   C
Cleaving the sky,
F   C7   Dm B♭
Sun, moon, and stars forgot,
F/C C7   F
Up - ward I'll fly,
      B♭/F F
Still all   my song shall be,
      B♭/F F   C
Nearer,   my God, to Thee.
F   B♭
Nearer, my God, to Thee,
F/C C7   F
Nearer to Thee.

O Come All Ye Faithful

Traditional

Verse 1

G   D
O come all ye faithful,
G D G   C G   D
Joyful, and triumphant,
 Em D A D
O come ye, O come ye,
G D   A7 D
To Bethle - hem.
G   D7 G D7 G
Come and behold Him,
D   G C   Am D
Born the King of   angels.

Refrain

G   D G D G
O come, let us a - dore Him,
      D G D7 G   D
O come, let us a - dore Him,
G D7   G D A7 D   G   C
O come, let us a - dore Him,___
G   D7 G
Christ the Lord.

Verse 2

G   D
Sing, choirs of angels,
G   D G C   G D
Sing in ex - ul - ta - tion,
 Em D   A D
O sing, all ye citizens,
G D   A7 D
Of heaven above!
G D7 G D7 G
Glory   to God___
     D G C Am D
All glory in the   highest.

Copyright © 2008 Amsco Publications, a Division of Music Sales Corporation.
All Rights Reserved. International Copyright Secured.

Refrain

    G   **D G D G**
O come, let us a - dore Him,
      D G D7 G   **D**
O come, let us a - dore Him,
G D7 **G D A7 D** **G** **C**
O come, let us a - dore Him,__
G   **D7 G**
Christ the Lord.

Verse 3

G   **D**
Child, for us sinners,
G   **D** **G C** **G** **D**
Poor and in the manger,
Em D   **A D**
We   would embrace thee,
G   **D**   **A7 D**
With love and awe,
G **D7**   **G** **D7** **G**
Who would not love Thee,
    D G C Am **D**
Loving us so dear - ly?

Refrain

    G   **D G D G**
O come, let us a - dore Him,
      D G D7 G   **D**
O come, let us a - dore Him,
G D7 **G D A7 D** **G** **C**
O come, let us a - dore Him,__
G   **D7 G**
Christ the Lord.

Verse 4

G　　　　　D
Yea, Lord, we greet Thee,
G　　D　G　C　G　　D
Born this happy morning,
Em　D　A　　D
Jesus, to Thee be,
G　D　A7　D
All glory　giv'n,
G　　D7　G　D7　G
Word of　the Fa - ther,
　　　D　G　C　　Am　D
Now in the flesh ap - pearing.

Refrain

　　G　　D　G　D　G
O come, let us a - dore Him,
　　　　D　G　D7　G　　D
O come, let us a - dore Him,
G　D7　G　D　A7　D　　G　　C
O come, let us a - dore Him,__
G　　D7　G
Christ the Lord.

O God Our Help In Ages Past

Words by Isaac Watts

Music by William Croft

Verse 1

    C   F C   Am F G C
O God, our help in   a - ges past,
    Am Em Am D G
Our hope for   years to come,
    C F Dm G C F E
Our shelter from the stormy blast,
    C   F C Dm G C
And our e - ter - nal home.

Verse 2

    C F C   Am F G   C
Under the shadow of Thy throne,
    Am Em Am D G
Thy saints have dwelt secure,
    C F   Dm G   C F E
Sufficient is   Thine arm a - lone,
    C   F   C Dm G C
And our defense is sure.

Verse 3

    C   F   C   Am F G C
Before the hills in   order stood,
    Am Em Am   D G
Or earth re - ceived her frame,
    C F Dm G   C   F E
From ev - erlast - ing Thou art God,
    C F C   Dm G C
To endless years the same.

Verse 4

    C   F   C   Am F   G C
Thy Word commands our flesh to dust,
    Am Em Am D G
"Return, ye sons of men."
    C F Dm G   C   F E
All nations rose from earth at first,
    C   F   C Dm G C
And turn to earth a - gain.

Copyright © 2008 Amsco Publications, a Division of Music Sales Corporation.
All Rights Reserved. International Copyright Secured.

Verse 5

   C   F   C Am F G   C
A thousand a - ges in Thy sight,
  Am Em Am D G
Are like an   evening gone,
    C F Dm G   C   F E
Short as the watch that ends the night,
C F   C Dm G C
Before the ris - ing sun.

Verse 6

    C F C   Am F G C
Time, like an ev - er   rolling stream,
   Am Em Am D G
Bears all its   sons a - way,
    C   F Dm G C F E
They fly, forgot - ten, as a dream,
C   F C Dm G C
Dies at the opening day.

Verse 7

    C   F C   Am F G   C
Like flowery fields the na - tions stand,
   Am Em Am D G
Pleased with the morning light,
    C   F Dm G C F   E
The flowers beneath the mower's hand,
C F   C Dm G C
Lie withering ere 'tis night.

Verse 8

   C   F C   Am F G C
O God, our help in   a - ges past,
   Am Em Am D G
Our hope for   years to come,
   C F Dm G C F E
Our shelter from the stormy blast,
C   F   C Dm G C
And our e - ter - nal home.

O Holy Night

Words by John Sullivan Dwight
Music by Adolphe Adam

Verse 1

C   F   C
O holy night, the stars are brightly shining.
                    G7   C
It is the night of the dear Savior's birth.
                   F   C C7
Long lay the world in sin and error pining,
          Em   B7   Em
Till He appeared and the soul felt its worth.
 G7   C
A thrill of hope, the weary soul rejoices,
  G7   C
For yonder breaks the new and glorious morn.
Am   Em   Dm   Am
Fall on your knees, O hear the angel voices!
 C G7   C F   C   G7   C
O night___ divine,_ O night when Christ was born.
 G7 C   Dm C   G7   C
O holy night, holy night, night divine!

Verse 2

C   F   C
Led by the light of faith serenely beaming,
                      G7   C
With glowing hearts by His cradle we stand.
                F   C   C7
So led by light of a star sweetly gleaming,
              Em   B7   Em
Here came the wise men from Orient land.
     G7   C
The King of kings lay thus in lowly manger,
  G7   C
In all our trials born to be our Friend.
Am   Em   Dm   Am
He knows our need, to our weakness is no stranger.
 C G7 C   F C   G7   C
Behold your King; before Him lowly bend!
 G7 C   Dm C   G7   C
Behold your King; before Him lowly bend!

Copyright © 2008 Amsco Publications, a Division of Music Sales Corporation.
All Rights Reserved. International Copyright Secured.

Verse 3

C   F   C

Truly He taught us to love one another.

                  G7   C

His law is love and His Gospel is peace.

                          F   C C7

Chains shall He break for the slave is our brother,

        Em   B7   Em

And in His Name all oppression shall cease.

    G7   C

Sweet hymns of joy in grateful chorus raise we,

    G7   C

Let all within us praise His holy Name,

Am   Em   Dm   Am

Christ is the Lord! O praise His name forever.

    C   G7 C   F   C   G7   C

His pow'r and glory evermore pro - claim,

    G7   C   Dm   C   G7   C

His pow'r and glory evermore pro - claim.

O Little Town Of Bethlehem

Words by Phillips Brooks
Music by Lewis H. Redner

Verse 1

G   Am
O little town of Bethlehem,
G   D7   G
How still we see thee lie.
G   G7 E7   Am
Above thy deep and dreamless sleep,
G   D7   G
The silent stars go by.
Am C#°   B B7
Yet in thy dark streets shineth,
E B7 G Am B7
The ever - lasting   light;
G   Am
The hopes and fears of all the years,
C#° G A7 D7   G
Are met in   thee tonight.

Verse 2

G   Am
For Christ is born of Mary,
G   D7 G
And gathered all above,
G   G7 E7   Am
While mortals sleep, the angels keep,
G   D7   G
Their watch of wondering love.
Am C#° B B7
O morning stars to - ge - ther,
E   B7 G   Am B7
Proclaim the ho - ly   birth,
G   Am
And praises sing to God, the King,
C#° G   A7 D7   G
And peace to   men on earth.

Copyright © 2008 Amsco Publications, a Division of Music Sales Corporation.
All Rights Reserved. International Copyright Secured.

Verse 3

   G   Am
How silently, how silently,
   G   D7 G
The wondrous gift is giv'n.
  G G7 E7 Am
So God imparts to human hearts,
   G   D7 G
The blessings of His Heav'n.
      Am C#° B B7
No ear may hear His coming,
  E B7 G Am B7
But in this world of sin,
    G   Am
Where meek souls will receive Him still,
C#° G A7 D7 G
The dear Christ enters in.

Verse 4

    G   Am
O holy Child of Bethlehem,
    G   D7 G
Descend to us, we pray.
    G G7 E7   Am
Cast out our sin, and enter in,
    G   D7 G
Be born in us today.
     Am C#° B B7
We hear the Christmas angels,
    E B7 G Am B7
The great glad tidings tell.
    G   Am
O come to us, abide with us,
C#° G A7 D7 G
Our Lord Em - manuel!

Oh, Susanna

Words and Music by Stephen Foster

Verse 1

    G
I came from Alabama,
            D
With my banjo on my knee,
     G
And I'm goin' to Louisiana,
     D7 **G**
My true love for to see.

It rained all night the day I left,
        A7   **D**
The weather it was dry,
    G
The sun so hot I froze to death,
      D   **G**
Susanna, don't you cry.

Refrain

    C   **G**
Oh, Susanna, oh, don't you cry for me,
   G   **D7** **G**
I come from Alabama, with my banjo on my knee.

Verse 2

    G
I had a dream the other night,
       D
When everything was still,
  G
I thought I saw Susanna,
   D7   **G**
A-coming down the hill.

The buckwheat cake was in her mouth,
        A7   **D**
The tear was in her eye,
   G
Says I, I'm coming from the South,
     D   **G**
Susanna, don't you cry.

Copyright © 2008 Amsco Publications, a Division of Music Sales Corporation.
All Rights Reserved. International Copyright Secured.

Refrain

     C   **G**
Oh, Susanna, oh, don't you cry for me,
 G   **D7**   **G**
I come from Alabama, with my banjo on my knee.

Verse 3

        G
I soon will be in New Orleans,
              D
And then I'll look all 'round,
    G
And when I find Susanna,
       D7   **G**
I'll fall upon the ground.

But if I do not find her,
           A7   **D**
Dis darling I surely die,
    G
And when I'm dead and buried,
      D   **G**
Susanna, don't you cry.

Refrain

     C   **G**
Oh, Susanna, oh, don't you cry for me,
 G   **D7**   **G**
I come from Alabama, with my banjo on my knee.

Old Folks At Home

Words and Music by Stephen Foster

Verse 1

D   D7   G
Way down upon the Swanee River,
D   Bm7 A7
Far, far   away,
D   D7   G
There's where my heart is turning ever,
D   A7   D
There's where the old folks stay.
D D7   G
All up and down the whole creation,
D   Bm7 A7
Sad - ly I   roam,
D   D7   G
Still longing for the old plantation,
D   A7   D
And for the old folks at home.

Refrain

A7   D   G   D
All the world is sad and dreary, ev'rywhere I roam.
A7 D D7   G
   Oh darlings, how my heart grows weary,
D   A7   D
Far from the old folks at home.

Verse 2

D   D7   G
All 'round the little farm I wandered,
D   Bm7 A7
When I was young,
D   D7   G
Then many happy days I squandered,
D   A7   D
Many the songs I sung.
D   D7   G
When I was playing with my brother,
D   Bm7 A7
Happy was I,
D D7   G
Oh, take me to my kind old mother,
D   A7   D
There let me live and die.

Copyright © 2008 Amsco Publications, a Division of Music Sales Corporation.
All Rights Reserved. International Copyright Secured.

Refrain

    A7   **D**   **G**   **D**
All the world is sad and dreary, ev'rywhere I roam.
A7 D D7   **G**
    Oh darlings, how my heart grows weary,
D   **A7**   **D**
Far from the old folks at home.

Verse 3

D   **D7**   **G**
One little hut among the bushes,
  D   **Bm7 A7**
One that I love,
D   **D7**   **G**
Still sadly to my mem'ry rushes,
D   **A7**   **D**
No matter where I rove.
D   **D7**   **G**
When shall I see the bees a humming,
D   **Bm7**   **A7**
All 'round the comb?
D   **D7**   **G**
When shall I hear the banjo strumming,
D   **A7**   **D**
Down by my good old home?

Refrain

A7   **D**   **G**   **D**
All the world is sad and dreary, ev'rywhere I roam.
A7 D D7   **G**
    Oh darlings, how my heart grows weary,
D   **A7**   **D**
Far from the old folks at home.

The Old Rugged Cross

Words and Music by George Bennar

Verse 1

     C   F
On a hill far away stood an old rugged cross,
D   G   G7   C
The emblem of suff'ring and shame,
                                  F
And I love that old cross where the dearest and best,
D   G   G7   C
For a world of lost sinners was slain.

Refrain

      G7   C   C° F C
So I'll cherish the old rugged cross,_____
            F   C
Till my trophies at last I lay down,
                       F
I will cling to the old rugged cross,
      C   G7   C
And exchange it some day for a crown.

Verse 2

      C   F
Oh, that old rugged cross, so despised by the world,
D   G   G7   C
Has a wondrous attraction for me,
                              F
For the dear Lamb of God left His glory above,
D G   G7   C
To bear it to dark Calvary.

Refrain

      G7   C   C° F C
So I'll cherish the old rugged cross,_____
            F   C
Till my trophies at last I lay down,
                       F
I will cling to the old rugged cross,
      C   G7   C
And exchange it some day for a crown.

Copyright © 2008 Amsco Publications, a Division of Music Sales Corporation.
All Rights Reserved. International Copyright Secured.

Verse 3

       C   **F**

In that old rugged cross, stained with blood so divine,

F   **C**

A wondrous beauty I see,

                         F

For 'twas on that old cross Jesus suffered and died,

D G   **G7**   **C**

To pardon and sanctify me.

Refrain

       G7   **C**   **C°F C**

So I'll cherish the old rugged cross,_____

       F   **C**

Till my trophies at last I lay down,

                     F

I will cling to the old rugged cross,

    C   **G7**   **C**

And exchange it some day for a crown.

Verse 4

       C   **F**

To the old rugged cross I will ever be true,

F   **C**

Its shame and reproach gladly bear,

                     F

Then He'll call me some day to my home far away,

D   **G**   **G7**   **C**

Where His glory forever I'll share.

Refrain

       G7   **C**   **C°F C**

So I'll cherish the old rugged cross,_____

       F   **C**

Till my trophies at last I lay down,

                     F

I will cling to the old rugged cross,

    C   **G7**   **C**

And exchange it some day for a crown.

On The Banks Of The Wabash

Words and Music by Paul Dresser

Verse 1

        G   C   G   D7   G
'Round my Indiana homestead wave the cornfields,__
           G7   A7   D7   G
In the distance loom the woodlands, clear and cool.
                       C   G   D7 G
Oftentimes my thoughts revert, to scenes of childhood,__
           G7   A7   D7   G
Where I first received my lessons, nature's school.
    B7   Em
But one thing there is missing in the picture,
  A7   D7
Without her face it seems so incomplete.
 G   C   G D7 G
I long to see my mother in the doorway,__
            G7   A7   D7   G
As she stood there years ago, her boy to greet.

Refrain

       G   B7   C   E7
Oh, the moonlight's fair tonight along the Wabash,__
      Am   A7   D7
From the fields there comes the breath of new-mown hay.
          G   B7   C
Through the sycamores the candle lights are gleaming,
       G   A7   D7 G
On the banks of the Wabash, far away.

Copyright © 2008 Amsco Publications, a Division of Music Sales Corporation.
All Rights Reserved. International Copyright Secured.

Verse 2

      G   **C**   **G D7 G**
Many years have passed since I strolled by the ri - ver,__
          G7   **A7**   **D7**   **G**
Arm in arm, with sweetheart Mary by my side,
                 C   **G**   **D7 G**
It was there I tried to tell her that I loved her,__
        G7   **A7**   **D7**   **G**
It was there I begged of her to be my bride.
    B7   **Em**
Long years have passed since I strolled through the churchyard.
   A7   **D7**
She's sleeping there, my angel, Mary dear,
 G   **C**   **G**   **D7 G**
I loved her, but she thought I didn't mean it,____
           G7   **A7**   **D7**   **G**
Still I'd give my future were she only here.

Refrain

       G   **B7**   **C**   **E7**
Oh, the moonlight's fair tonight along the Wabash,__
       Am   **A7**   **D7**
From the fields there comes the breath of new-mown hay.
     G   **B7**   **C**
Through the sycamores the candle lights are gleaming,
    G   **A7**   **D7** **G**
On the banks of the Wabash, far away.

Old Hundredth (The Doxology)

Words by Thomas Ken
Music by Louis Bourgeois

F   Dm Am B♭   F Dm C   F
Praise God, from Whom all blessings flow,

     Dm F C Dm Gm F   C
Praise Him, all creatures here be - low,

Dm   C   F C   F B♭   C F
Praise Him a - bove, the heav'nly host,

C   F Dm Gm Gm7 F C F
Praise Father, Son, and   Holy Ghost.

Copyright © 2008 Amsco Publications, a Division of Music Sales Corporation.
All Rights Reserved. International Copyright Secured.

Onward, Christian Soldiers

Words by Sabine Baring-Gould
Music by Arthur Sullivan

Verse 1

    F   **C7**   **F**
Onward, Christian soldiers, marching as to war,
                     C7   **G7**   **C**
With the cross of Jesus, going on before.
                        F   **B♭**
Christ, the royal Master, leads against the foe;
                           F♯° **Gm** **G7** **C7**
Forward into battle, see His ban - ners go.

Refrain

    F   **C7**
Onward, Christian soldiers,
                      F
Marching as to war,
         Gm7   **F**
With the cross of Jesus,
B♭ G7 C7 F
Going on before.

Verse 2

    F   **C7**   **F**
At the sign of triumph Satan's host doth flee;
                     C7   **G7**   **C**
On then, Christian soldiers, on to victory.
                       F   **B♭**
Hell's foundations quiver at the shout of praise;
                         F♯° **Gm** **G7**   **C7**
Brothers lift your voices, loud your an - thems raise.

Refrain

    F   **C7**
Onward, Christian soldiers,
                      F
Marching as to war,
         Gm7   **F**
With the cross of Jesus,
B♭ G7 C7 F
Going on before.

Copyright © 2008 Amsco Publications, a Division of Music Sales Corporation.
All Rights Reserved. International Copyright Secured.

Verse 3

      F   **C7**   **F**

Like a mighty army, moves the church of God;

              C7   **G7**   **C**

Brothers, we are treading where the saints have trod.

                  F   **B♭**

We are not divided, all one body we,

                            F♯° Gm G7 C7

One in hope and doctrine, one in   charity.

Refrain

      F   **C7**

Onward, Christian soldiers,

                    F

Marching as to war,

         Gm7   **F**

With the cross of Jesus,

B♭ G7 C7   **F**

Going on before.

Verse 4

      F   **C7**   **F**

Crowns and thrones may perish, kingdoms rise and wane,

                  C7   **G7**

But the church of Jesus, constant will remain.

                  F   **B♭**

Gates of hell can never, 'gainst that church prevail;

                          F♯° Gm G7   **C7**

We have Christ's own promise, and that cannot fail.

Refrain

      F   **C7**

Onward, Christian soldiers,

                    F

Marching as to war,

         Gm7   **F**

With the cross of Jesus,

B♭ G7 C7   **F**

Going on before.

186

Verse 5

F   C7   F

What the saints established that I hold for true.

                  C7   G7   C

What the saints believed, that I believe too.

           F   Bb

Long as earth endureth, men the faith will hold,

                           F#° Gm G7   C7

Kingdoms, nations, empires, in   de - struction rolled.

Refrain

F   C7

Onward, Christian soldiers,

                F

Marching as to war,

      Gm7 F

With the cross of Jesus,

Bb G7 C7   F

Going on before.

Verse 6

F   C7   F

Onward, then ye, people, join our happy throng,

                  C7   G7   C

Blend with ours your voices in the triumph song.

           F   Bb

Glory, laud and honor unto Christ the King,

                           F#° Gm G7   C7

This through countless ages, men and   angels sing.

Refrain

F   C7

Onward, Christian soldiers,

                F

Marching as to war,

      Gm7   F

With the cross of Jesus,

Bb G7 C7   F

Going on before.

The Pledge Of Allegiance

I Pledge Allegiance

To the Flag

Of the United States of America,

And to the Republic

For Which It Stands,

One Nation

Under God,

Indivisible,

With Liberty

And Justice

For All.

Copyright © 2008 Amsco Publications, a Division of Music Sales Corporation.
All Rights Reserved. International Copyright Secured.

Prayer Of Thanksgiving

Traditional

Verse 1

    C   G7   C
We gather together to ask the Lord's blessing,
   G   Am D7 G C   D7   G
He chastens and has - tens his will to make known.
    G7   C   G7   C
The wicked oppressing, cease them from distressing,
C7 F   C   Dm7 G7   C
Sing praise to his name, he forgets   not his own.

Verse 2

    C   G7   C
Beside us to guide us, our God with us joining,
   G   Am D7 G C   D7 G
Ordaining, maintain - ing his kingdom di - vine.
    G7   C   G7   C
So from the beginning the fight we were winning;
C7   F   C   Dm7 G7 C
Thou, Lord, wast at our side, all glory be Thine.

Verse 3

    C   G7   C
We all do extol Thee, Thou leader triumphant,
   G   Am D7 G C   D7 G
And pray that Thou still our defender wilt be.
    G7   C   G7   C
Let thy congregation escape tribulation!
C7 F   C   Dm7 G7   C
Thy name be ever praised! O Lord, make us free!

Copyright © 2008 Amsco Publications, a Division of Music Sales Corporation.
All Rights Reserved. International Copyright Secured.

Ragtime Cowboy Joe

Words and Music by Lewis F. Muir, Grant Clarke, and Maurice Abrahams

Verse 1

    C   **F**   **C**   **F**
Out in Arizona where the bad men are,
        C   **F**   **D7**   **G7**
And the only friend to guide you is an evening star,___
    C   **F**   **C**   **F**
The roughest, toughest man by far,_
D7   **G7**   **C**
Is Ragtime Cowboy Joe.
G   **C**   **G**   **C**
Got his name from singing to the cows and sheep,
G   **E**   **A7** **D7** **G**
Ev'ry night they say he sings the herd to sleep,
C   **F** **C**   **F**
In a basso rich and deep,
G7   **B7**   **G7**
Croonin' soft and low.

Refrain

          C
He always sings raggy music to the cattle,
        G
As he swings back and forward in the saddle,
        G
On a horse that is syncopated gaited,
           C
And there's such a funny meter,
      G   **G7**
To the roar of his repeater.
        C
How they run when they hear that fellow's gun,
        D7
Because the western folks all know,
    F
He's a high-falutin', rootin' tootin' son-of-a-gun,
        D7   **G7**   **C**
From Arizona, Ragtime Cowboy Joe.

Copyright © 2008 Amsco Publications, a Division of Music Sales Corporation.
All Rights Reserved. International Copyright Secured.

Verse 2

```
           C                 F            C       F
Dressed up ev'ry Sunday in his Sunday clothes,
           C              F              D7     G7
He beats it to the village where he always goes,
             C    F    C              F
And ev'ry girl in town is Joe's,__
             D7   G7    C
'Cause he's a ragtime bear.
G                  C              G        C
When he starts a-moving on the dance hall floor,
G                E              A7  D7 G
No one but a lunatic would start a   war,
C                    F  C   F
Wise men know his forty four,
G7          B7        G7
Makes men dance for sure.
```

Refrain

```
              C
He always sings raggy music to the cattle,
        G
As he swings back and forward in the saddle,
        G
On a horse that is syncopated gaited,
              C
And there's such a funny meter,
            G             G7
To the roar of his repeater.
            C
How they run when they hear that fellow's gun,
                  D7
Because the western folks all know,
        F
He's a high-falutin', rootin' tootin' son-of-a-gun,
              D7      G7      C
From Arizona, Ragtime Cowboy Joe.
```

Rally Round The Flag

Words and Music by George F. Root

Verse 1

         G   D7   **Em**
Yes, we'll rally round the flag, boys,
       B7   **C**
We'll rally once again,
G   **A7 D7**
Shouting the battle cry of freedom;
         G   **Em**
We will rally from the hillside,
        B7   **C**
We'll gather from the plain,
G   **D7 G**
Shouting the battle cry of freedom.

Refrain

         G
The Union forever, Hurrah! boys, Hurrah!
          A7/E D7
Bright in its glory shines ev'ry star,
     G   **D7**   **Em**
While we rally round the flag, boys,
   D7   **C**
Rally once again,
G   **D7 G**
Shouting the battle cry of freedom.

Verse 2

         G   **D7**   **Em**
We are springing to the call,
      B7   **C**
Of our brothers gone before,
G   **A7 D7**
Shouting the battle cry of freedom;
        G   **Em**
And we'll fill the vacant ranks,
      B7   **C**
With a million patriots more;
G   **D7 G**
Shouting the battle cry of freedom.

Copyright © 2008 Amsco Publications, a Division of Music Sales Corporation.
All Rights Reserved. International Copyright Secured.

Refrain

    G
The Union forever, Hurrah! boys, Hurrah!
            A7/E D7
Bright in its glory shines ev'ry star,
      G   **D7**   **Em**
While we rally round the flag, boys,
   D7   **C**
Rally once again,
G   **D7 G**
Shouting the battle cry of freedom.

Verse 3

      G   **D7** **Em**
We will welcome to our numbers,
B7   **C**
The loyal, true and brave,
G   **A7** **D7**
Shouting the battle cry of freedom;
        G   **Em**
And although they may be poor,
      B7 **C**
Not a man shall be a slave,
G   **D7 G**
Shouting the battle cry of freedom.

Refrain

    G
The Union forever, Hurrah! boys, Hurrah!
            A7/E D7
Bright in its glory shines ev'ry star,
      G   **D7**   **Em**
While we rally round the flag, boys,
   D7   **C**
Rally once again,
G   **D7 G**
Shouting the battle cry of freedom.

Red River Valley

Traditional

Verse 1

       D   **A7**   **D**
Come and sit by my side, if you love me,
                     A7
Do not hasten to bid me adieu,
   D   **G**
But remember the Red River Valley,
A7   **D**
And the cowboy that loves you so true.

Verse 2

       D   **A7**   **D**
Won't you think of this valley you're leaving?
                 D
Oh, how lonely, how sad it will be,
 D   **G**
Oh, think of the fond hearts you're breaking,
A7   **D**
And the grief you are causing me.

Verse 3

      D   **A7**   **D**
From this valley they say you are going,
                 A7
When you go, may your darling go too?
    D   **G**
Would you leave me behind unprotected,
  A7   **D**
When she loves no other but you?

Copyright © 2008 Amsco Publications, a Division of Music Sales Corporation.
All Rights Reserved. International Copyright Secured.

Verse 4

      D   **A7**
I have promised you, darling,

      D   **A7**
That never will a word from my lips cause you pain,

      D   **G**
And my life, it will be yours forever,

    A7   **D**
If you only will love me again.

Verse 5

       D   **A7**   **D**
I've been thinking a long time, my darling,

                          A7
Of the sweet words you never would say,

    D   **G**
Now, alas, must my fond hopes all vanish,

    A7   **D**
For they say you are going away.

Verse 6

     D   **A7**   **D**
They will bury me where you have wandered,

                       A7
Near the hills where the daffodils grow,

           D   **G**
When you're gone from the Red River Valley,

    A7   **D**
For I can't live without you I know.

Rock Of Ages

Words by Augustus M. Toplady
Music by Thomas Hastings

Verse 1

        C   F   C
Rock of Ages, cleft for me,
          G   C
Let me hide myself in Thee,
        G7   C
Let the water and the blood,
        G7   C
From Thy wounded side that flowed,
           F   C
Be of sin the double cure,
Am   C/G   G7   C
Cleanse me from its guilt and pow'r.

Verse 2

        C   F   C
Not the labor of my hands,
           G   C
Can fulfill Thy law's demands,
        G7   C
Could my zeal no respite know,
        G7   C
Could my tears forever flow,
         F   C
All for sin could not atone,
Am   C/G   G7   C
Thou must save, and Thou alone.

Verse 3

        C   F   C
Nothing in my hand I bring,
          G   C
Simply to the cross I cling,
        G7   C
Naked, come to Thee for dress,
        G7   C
Helpless look to Thee for grace,
         F   C
Foul, I to the fountain fly,
Am   C/G   G7 C
Wash me, Savior, or I die.

Copyright © 2008 Amsco Publications, a Division of Music Sales Corporation.
All Rights Reserved. International Copyright Secured.

Verse 4

        C   **F**   **C**
While I draw this fleeting breath,
            G   **C**
When mine eyelids close in death,
    G7   **C**
When I soar to worlds unknown,
    G7   **C**
See Thee on Thy judgment throne,
            F   **C**
Rock of Ages, cleft for me,
Am   **C/G**   **G7**   **C**
Let me hide myself in Thee.

Rock-A My Soul

Traditional

Refrain

        D   **G/D Dmaj7**   **G/D**
I'm gonna rock-a my soul in the bosom of A - braham,
A7
Rock-a my soul in the bosom of Abraham,
Dmaj7   **G/D**   **D**   **F#°**
Rock-a my soul_____ in the bosom of A - braham,
A7 D/A A   **D**
Oh,   rock-a my soul.

Verse 1

     D9   **D**   **D9**   **D**
When I went down to the valley to pray,
D9   **C/G D/F#**
Oh, rock-a my soul._____
   D9   **C/G**   **D9**
My soul got happy and I stayed all day,
   A7   **D** **G6 F/A**
Oh, rock-a my soul._____

Refrain

        D   **G/D Dmaj7**   **G/D**
I'm gonna rock-a my soul in the bosom of A - braham,
A7
Rock-a my soul in the bosom of Abraham,
Dmaj7   **G/D**   **D**   **F#°**
Rock-a my soul_____ in the bosom of A - braham,
A7 D/A A   **D**
Oh,   rock-a my soul.

Verse 2

     D9   **D**   **D9**   **D**
When I came home from the valley at night,
D9   **C/G D/F#**
Oh, rock-a my soul._____
   D9   **C/G**   **D9**
I knew that ev'rything would be all right,
   A7   **D** **G6 F/A**
Oh, rock-a my soul._____

Copyright © 2008 Amsco Publications, a Division of Music Sales Corporation.
All Rights Reserved. International Copyright Secured.

       D   **G/D Dmaj7**   **G/D**

I'm gonna rock-a my soul in the bosom of A - braham,

A7

Rock-a my soul in the bosom of Abraham,

Dmaj7   **G/D**   **D**   **F#°**

Rock-a my soul_____ in the bosom of A - braham,

A7 D/A A   **D**

Oh,   rock-a my soul.

    D9   **D**   **D9**   **D**

I felt so sad on the morning before,

Verse 3   **D9**   **C/G D/F#**

Oh, rock-a my soul._____

    D9   **C/G**   **D9**

I found the peace that I was looking for,

      A7   **D G6 F/A**

Oh, rock-a my soul._____

       D   **G/D Dmaj7**   **G/D**

I'm gonna rock-a my soul in the bosom of A - braham,

Refrain   **A7**

Rock-a my soul in the bosom of Abraham,

Dmaj7   **G/D**   **D**   **F#°**

Rock-a my soul_____ in the bosom of A - braham,

A7 D/A A   **D**

Oh,   rock-a my soul.

Sailing, Sailing

Words and Music by Godfrey Marks

Verse 1

        G
Y'heave ho! my lads, the wind blows free,
 D7
A pleasant gale is on our lee,
     G
And soon across the ocean clear,
      D   **A7**   **D**
Our gallant bark shall bravely steer.
 D7   **G**
But ere we part from England's shores tonight,
 D7   **G**
A song we'll sing for home and beauty bright.

Refrain

Em   **B7**
Then here's to the sailor,
   C   **G**
And here's to the hearts so true,
                   B7
Who will think of him upon the waters blue.
G   **C**   **G**
Sailing, sailing over the bounding main,
   D7   **G**   **Em**
For many a stormy wind shall blow,
   D   **A7**   **D**
Ere Jack comes home again.
G   **C**   **G**
Sailing, sailing over the bounding main,
 C   **B7**   **Em**   **A7**
For many a stormy wind shall blow,
    G   **A7**   **D**
Ere Jack comes home again.

Copyright © 2008 Amsco Publications, a Division of Music Sales Corporation.
All Rights Reserved. International Copyright Secured.

Verse 2

    G
The sailor's life is bold and free,
  D7
His home is on the rolling sea,
    G
And never heart more true or brave,
    D   **A7**   **D**
Than he who launches on the wave.
D7   **G**
Afar he speeds in distant climes to roam;
   D7   **G**
With jocund song he rides the sparkling foam.

Refrain

Em   **B7**
Then here's to the sailor,
   C   **G**
And here's to the hearts so true,
                       B7
Who will think of him upon the waters blue.
G   **C**   **G**
Sailing, sailing over the bounding main,
  D7   **G**   **Em**
For many a stormy wind shall blow,
   D   **A7**   **D**
Ere Jack comes home again.
G   **C**   **G**
Sailing, sailing over the bounding main,
  C   **B7**   **Em**   **A7**
For many a stormy wind shall blow,
  G   **A7**   **D**
Ere Jack comes home again.

Verse 3

      G
The tide is flowing with the gale,
      D7
Y'heave ho! my lads, set every sail.
      G
The harbor bar we soon shall clear,
     D   A7   D
Farewell once more to home so dear;
    D7   G
For when the tempest rages loud and long,
    D7   G
That home shall be our guiding star among.

Refrain

    Em   B7
Then here's to the sailor,
     C   G
And here's to the hearts so true,
                       B7
Who will think of him upon the waters blue.
G   C   G
Sailing, sailing over the bounding main,
    D7   G   Em
For many a stormy wind shall blow,
    D   A7   D
Ere Jack comes home again.
G   C   G
Sailing, sailing over the bounding main,
   C   B7   Em   A7
For many a stormy wind shall blow,
    G   A7   D
Ere Jack comes home again.

Sourwood Mountain

Traditional

Verse 1

E   A   E
Chickens a crowin' on Sourwood Mountain,
     B7 E
Hey, hey, diddle um day.
        A E
So many pretty girls I can't count 'em,
     B7 E
Hey, hey, diddle um day.
A   E
So many girls I just can't count 'em,
B7   E
So many girls on Sourwood Mountain,
A   E
So many girls on Sourwood Mountain,
    B7 E
Hey, hey, diddle um day.

Verse 2

E   A E
I call my darling a blue eyed daisy,
    B7 E
Hey, hey, diddle um day.
       A   E
If she won't have me, I'll sure go crazy,
    B7 E
Hey, hey, diddle um day.
A   E
I've got to have my blue eyed daisy,
B7   E
If she refuses, I'll go crazy,
A   E
I've got to have my blue eyed daisy,
    B7 E
Hey, hey, diddle um day.

Copyright © 2008 Amsco Publications, a Division of Music Sales Corporation.
All Rights Reserved. International Copyright Secured.

Verse 3

E   A E
Ducks go a-swimming across the river,
    B7 E
Hey, hey, diddle um day.
     A   E
And in winter, we sure do shiver,
   B7 E
Hey, hey, diddle um day.
A   E
Ducks go a-swimming across the river,
B7   E
And in winter, we sure do shiver,
A   E
I like living on Sourwood Mountain,
   B7 E
Hey, hey, diddle um day.

Verse 4

E   A   E
My true love lives at the head of the holler,
   B7 E
Hey, hey, diddle um day.
      A   E
She won't come and I won't foller,
   B7 E
Hey, hey, diddle um day.
A   E
My true love lives at the head of the holler,
B7   E
She won't come and I won't foller.
A   E
My true love lives at the head of the holler,
   B7 E
Hey, hey, diddle um day.

Verse 5

```
        E               A       E
My true love lives over the river,
           B7        E
Hey, hey, diddle um day.
                       A       E
A few more steps and I'll be with her,
           B7        E
Hey, hey, diddle um day.
A                 E
My true love lives over the river,
B7                E
A few more steps and I'll be with her,
A                 E
My true love lives over the river,
           B7      E
Hey, hey, diddle um day.
```

Verse 6

```
        E               A       E
Ducks in the pond, geese in the ocean,
           B7        E
Hey, hey, diddle um day.
                          A       E
Devil's in the women, if they take a notion,
           B7        E
Hey, hey, diddle um day.
A                 E
Ducks in the pond, geese in the ocean,
B7                     E
Devil's in the women, if they take a notion,
A                 E
Ducks in the pond, geese in the ocean,
           B7      E
Hey, hey, diddle um day.
```

St. Louis Blues

Words and Music by W.C. Handy

Verse 1

  G7   **C7**   **G7**
I hate to see the evenin' sun go down,
C7   **G**
Hate to see the evenin' sun go down,
D7   **G**
'Cause my baby, he done left this town.
               C7   **G7**
Feelin' tomorrow, like I feel today,
C   **C7**   **G7**
Feel tomorrow, like I feel today,
D7   **G**
I'll pack my trunk, and make my getaway.
      Gm
St. Louis woman,
Cm   **C#°7** **D7**
With her diamond rings,

Pulls that man around,
      Gm
By her apron strings.
               C#°7 **D7**
'Tweren't for powder and for store-bought hair,
               Gm **A7** **D**
The man I love would not go nowhere, no - where.

Copyright © 2008 Amsco Publications, a Division of Music Sales Corporation.
All Rights Reserved. International Copyright Secured.

Refrain

G
Got the St. Louis blues,
                         C G C G C G
Just as blue as I can be,_____
  C
That man got a heart,
              G   **C G C G C G**
Like a rock cast in the sea,_____
                     D7   **G**
Or else he wouldn't have gone so far from me.
G
I love that man,
                            C G C G C G
Like a schoolboy loves his pie,_____
    C
Like a Kentucky Colonel,
              G   **C G C G C G**
Loves his mint and rye,_____
             D7   **G**
I'll love my baby till the day I die.

Scarborough Fair

Traditional

Verse 1

Em   Bm   G   Bm
Are you going to Scarborough Fair?
Em   C♯m7♭5 Em   Bm
Parsley, sage, rosemary and thyme,
        A   Em   D
Remember me to a bonny lass there,
   G   D   B   Em
For once she was a true love of mine.

Verse 2

        Bm   G   Bm
Tell her to make me a cambric shirt,
Em   C♯m7♭5 Em   Bm
Parsley, sage, rosemary and thyme,
      A   Em   D
Without any needle or thread work'd in it,
   G   D   B   Em
And she shall be a true love of mine.

Verse 3

       Bm   G   Bm
Tell her to wash it in yonder well,
Em   C♯m7♭5 Em   Bm
Parsley, sage, rosemary and thyme,
        A   Em   D
Where water ne'er sprung, nor drop of rain fell,
   G   D   B   Em
And she shall be a true love of mine.

Verse 4

      Bm   G   Bm
Tell her to plough me an acre of land,
Em   C♯m7♭5 Em   Bm
Parsley, sage, rosemary and thyme,
      A   Em   D
Between the sea and the salt sea strand,
   G   D   B   Em
And she shall be a true love of mine.

Copyright © 2008 Amsco Publications, a Division of Music Sales Corporation.
All Rights Reserved. International Copyright Secured.

Verse 5

                   Bm   **G**   **Bm**
Tell her to plough it with one ram's horn,
Em   **C♯m7♭5** **Em**   **Bm**
Parsley, sage, rosemary and thyme,
                 A   **Em**   **D**
And sow it all over with one peppercorn,
       G   **D**   **B**   **Em**
And she shall be a true love of mine.

Verse 6

                   Bm   **G**   **Em**
Tell her to reap it with a sickle of leather,
Em   **C♯m7♭5** **Em**   **Bm**
Parsley, sage, rosemary and thyme,
                A   **Em**   **D**
And tie it all up with a tom-tit's feather,
       G   **D**   **B**   **Em**
And she shall be a true love of mine.

Verse 7

                   Bm   **G**   **Bm**
Tell her to gather it all in a sack,
Em   **C♯m7♭5** **Em**   **Bm**
Parsley, sage, rosemary and thyme,
                A   **Em**   **D**
And carry it home on a butterfly's back,
       G   **D**   **B**   **Em**
And she shall be a true love of mine.

She Wore A Yellow Ribbon

Words and Music by George A. Norton

Verse 1

       D
'Round her neck, she wore a yellow ribbon,

She wore it in the springtime,
   E7   **A7**
And in the month of May.
   D
And if you asked her,

Why the heck she wore it,
                     A7   **D**
She'd say, "It's for my lover, who is far, far away."

Chorus

    G   **D**
Far away, far away,
                 A7
She wore it for her lover far away.
D
'Round her neck she wore a yellow ribbon.
                 A7 **D**
She wore it for her lover who is far, far away.

Verse 2

'Round the block she pushed a baby carriage,

She pushed it in the springtime,
   E7   **A7**
And in the month of May.
   D
And if you asked her,

Why the heck she wore it,
                 A7   **D**
She'd say, "It's for my lover, who is far, far away."

Copyright © 2008 Amsco Publications, a Division of Music Sales Corporation.
All Rights Reserved. International Copyright Secured.

Chorus
        G   **D**
Far away, far away,
                       A7
She wore it for her lover far away.
D
'Round her neck she wore a yellow ribbon.
                       A7 D
She wore it for her lover who is far, far away.

Verse 3
Around her thigh she wore a yellow garter,

She wore it in the springtime,
     E7   **A7**
And in the month of May.
     D
And if you asked her,

Why the heck she wore it,
                       A7   **D**
She'd say, "It's for my lover, who is far, far away."

Chorus
        G   **D**
Far away, far away,
                       A7
She wore it for her lover far away.
D
'Round her neck she wore a yellow ribbon.
                       A7 D
She wore it for her lover who is far, far away.

She'll Be Comin' Round The Mountain

Traditional

Verse 1

      G
She'll be comin' round the mountain when she comes,
                      A7   **D7**
She'll be comin' round the mountain when she comes,
      G   **G7**
She'll be steamin' and a-puffin',
    C   **C#°**
Oh Lord, she won't stop for nothin',
    G   **A7**   **D7**   **G**
She'll be comin' round the mountain when she comes.

Verse 2

      G
She'll be drivin' six white horses when she comes,
                A7   **D7**
She'll be drivin' six white horses when she comes,
      G   **G7**
She'll be drivin' six white horses,
C   **C#°**
Drivin' six white horses,
    G   **A7**   **D7**   **G**
She'll be drivin' six white horses when she comes.

Verse 3

      G
Oh, we'll all go out and meet her when she comes,
                A7   **D7**
Oh, we'll all go out and meet her when she comes,
      G   **G7**
Oh, we'll all go out and meet her,
C   **C#°**
All go out and meet her,
    G   **A7**   **D7**   **G**
Oh, we'll all go out and meet her when she comes.

Copyright © 2008 Amsco Publications, a Division of Music Sales Corporation.
All Rights Reserved. International Copyright Secured.

Verse 4

        G
We will kill the old red rooster when she comes,
                            A7   **D7**
We will kill the old red rooster when she comes,
        G   **G7**
We will kill the old red rooster,
C   **C#°**
Kill the old red rooster,
        G   **A7**   **D7**   **G**
We will kill the old red rooster when she comes.

Verse 5

        G
We will all have chicken and dumplings when she comes,
                                A7   **D7**
We will all have chicken and dumplings when she comes,
        G   **G7**
We will all have chicken and dumplings,
C   **C#°**
All have chicken and dumplings,
        G   **A7**   **D7**   **G**
We will all have chicken and dumplings when she comes.

Shenandoah

Traditional

Verse 1

```
     D          Bm        D
Oh, Shenandoah   I long to hear you,
  G    Em        D
Away,     you rolling river,
F♯m  Bm         F♯m       G
   Oh, Shenandoah   I long to hear you,
D   Bm  G        D   G      D    A  D
   Away, I'm bound away, across the wide Missouri.
```

Verse 2

```
                Bm         D
Oh, Shenandoah   I love your daughter,
  G    Em         D
Away,     you rolling river,
   Bm       F♯m          G
For her I'd cross    your roaming water,
D   Bm  G        D   G      D    A  D
   Away, I'm bound away, across the wide Missouri.
```

Verse 3

```
               Bm          D
'Tis seven years    since I have seen you,
  G    Em        D
Away,     you rolling river,
F♯m  Bm        F♯m       G
   Oh, Shenandoah   I long to see you,
D   Bm  G        D   G      D    A  D
   Away, I'm bound away, across the wide Missouri.
```

Copyright © 2008 Amsco Publications, a Division of Music Sales Corporation.
All Rights Reserved. International Copyright Secured.

Verse 4

```
                      Bm            D
     Oh, Shenandoah    I'm bound to leave you,
        G    Em         D
     Away,    you rolling river,
     F♯m   Bm        F♯m        G
        Oh, Shenandoah    I'll not deceive you,
     D   Bm  G          D    G        D      A D
        Away, I'm bound away, across the wide Missouri.
```

Verse 5

```
                      Bm            D
     Oh, Shenandoah    I'll not forget you,
        G    Em         D
     Away,    you rolling river,
     F♯m   Bm        F♯m        G
        Oh, Shenandoah    you're in my mem'ry,
     D   Bm  G          D    G        D      A D
        Away, I'm bound away, across the wide Missouri.
```

Verse 6

```
                 D        Bm        D
     Oh, Shenandoah    I long to hear you,
        G    Em         D
     Away,    you rolling river,
     F♯m   Bm        F♯m        G
        Oh, Shenandoah    I long to hear you,
     D   Bm  G          D    G        D      A D
        Away, I'm bound away, across the wide Missouri.
```

The Sidewalks Of New York

Words and Music by Charles B. Lawlor & James W. Blake

Verse 1

$\begin{array}{ll} \text{G} & \text{D7} \end{array}$
East side, West side,
C   D7   G
All around the town,
    C   C#°   G
The tots sang "ring-a-rosie,"
E7   A7   D7
"London Bridge is falling down."
G   D7   G   G7
Boys and girls together,___
C   G   G7
Me and Mamie O'Rourke,___
    C   C#°   G
We tripped the light fantastic,
E7   A7   D7   G
On the sidewalks of New York.

Verse 2

G   D7
East side, West side,
C   D7   G
All around the town,
      C   C#°   G
Sweet Mamie grew up,
    E7   A7   D7
And bought herself a sweet little Alice-blue gown.
G   D7   G   G7
All the fellas dug her,___
      C   G   G7
You should have heard them squark,
    C   C#°   G
When I escorted Mamie,
E7   A7   D7   G
Round the sidewalks of New York.

Copyright © 2008 Amsco Publications, a Division of Music Sales Corporation.
All Rights Reserved. International Copyright Secured.

Verse 3

G   **D7**
East side, West side,
C   **D7**   **G**
Riding through the parks,
    C   **C♯°**   **G**
We started swinging at Jilly's,
      E7   **A7 D7**
Then we split to P.J. Clark's.
G   **D7**   **G**   **G7**
On to Chuck's Composite,___
      C   **G**   **G7**
Then a drink at The Stork,___
    C   **C♯°**   **G**
We won't get home until morning,
        C   **C♯°** **G**
'Cause we're going to take a walk,
E7   **A7**   **D7**   **G**
On the sidewalks of New York.

Silent Night

Words by Joseph Mohr
Music by Franz Xaver Gruber

Verse 1

D
Silent night, holy night,
A   **D**
All is calm, all is bright,
G   **D**
Round yon virgin mother and child.
G   **D**
Holy infant so tender and mild,
A   **A7**   **D**
Sleep in heavenly peace,
          A7   **D**
Sleep in heavenly peace.

Verse 2

D
Silent night, holy night,
A   **D**
Shepherds quake at the sight,
G   **D**
Glories stream from heaven afar.
G   **D**
Heavenly hosts sing Alleluia.
A   **A7**   **D**
Christ, the Savior is born,
          A7   **D**
Christ, the Savior is born!

Verse 3

D
Silent night, holy night,
A   **D**
Son of God, love's pure light,
G   **D**
Radiant beams from Thy holy face.
G   **D**
With the dawn of redeeming grace,
A **A7**   **D**
Jesus, Lord, at Thy birth,
    A7   **D**
Jesus, Lord, at Thy birth.

Copyright © 2008 Amsco Publications, a Division of Music Sales Corporation.
All Rights Reserved. International Copyright Secured.

Verse 4

D
Silent night, holy night,
A   **D**
Wondrous star, led thy light,
G   **D**
With the angels let us sing,
G   **D**
Alleluia to our King,
A   **A7**   **D**
Christ, the Savior is born,
        A7   **D**
Christ, the Savior is born!

The Soldier's Farewell

Words and Music by Johanna Kink

Verse 1

C   **G7sus4 G7**
Ah, love, how can I leave   thee?
C   **F/C C   C/G G**
The sad thought deep doth grieve me,
C   **C7 C/E Fsus4 F**
But know, whate'er be - falls   me,
D   **D7   D7/F♯ Gsus4 G**
I go where hon - or   calls me.

Refrain

G7 C
Farewell, farewell,
     F   **C**
My own true love!
  G7 C Fmaj7
Farewell, farewell,
D7/F♯ C/G G7 C
My   own true love.

Verse 2

C   **G7sus4 G7**
Ne'er more may I behold   thee,
C   **F/C C C/G G**
Or to my heart enfold thee;
C   **C7 C/E Fsus4 F**
In work array ap - pear - ing,
D   **D7   D7/F♯ Gsus4 G**
The foe's stern hosts are   near - ing.

Refrain

G7 C
Farewell, farewell,
     F   **C**
My own true love!
  G7 C Fmaj7
Farewell, farewell,
D7/F♯ C/G G7 C
My   own true love.

Copyright © 2008 Amsco Publications, a Division of Music Sales Corporation.
All Rights Reserved. International Copyright Secured.

Verse 3

C   G7sus4 G7
I think of thee with long - ing;
      C   F/C C   C/G G
Think thou, when tears are thronging,
C   C7 C/E Fsus4 F
That with my last feint sigh - ing,
D   D7 D7/F♯ Gsus4 G
I'll whisper soft, while dy - ing.

Refrain

G7 C
Farewell, farewell,
     F   C
My own true love!
     G7 C Fmaj7
Farewell, farewell,
D7/F♯ C/G G7 C
My   own true love.

Sometimes I Feel Like A Motherless Child

Traditional

Verse 1

Em
Sometimes I feel like a motherless child,
C   **Em**
Sometimes I feel like a motherless child,

Sometimes I feel like a motherless child,
C7 **E7**   **F♯m7♭5**
A long way from my home.
A7 **C7** **Em** **B7** **Em**
  A long way from home.
          C7 **Em**   **F♯m7♭5**
True believer, a long way from home,
A7 **C7** **Em** **B7** **Em**
  A long way from home.

Verse 2

Em
Sometimes I feel like I'm almost gone,
C   **Em**
Sometimes I feel like I'm almost gone,

Sometimes I feel like I'm almost gone,
C7   **E7**   **F♯m7♭5**
Way up in the heav'nly land,
A7 C7   **Em** **B7**   **Em**
  Way up in the heav'nly land,
          C7   **Em**   **F♯m7♭5**
True believer, way up in the heav'nly land,
A7 C7   **Em** **B7**   **Em**
  Way up in the heav'nly land,

Copyright © 2008 Amsco Publications, a Division of Music Sales Corporation.
All Rights Reserved. International Copyright Secured.

Em

Verse 3 Motherless children have a hard time,
C   **Em**
Motherless children have such a hard time,

Motherless children have such a really hard time,
   C7   E7   **F♯m7♭5**
A long way from my home.
A7   C7 Em B7   Em
   A long way from home.
                    C7   Em   **F♯m7♭5**
True believer, a long way from home,
A7   C7 Em B7   Em
   A long way from home.

Em

Verse 4 Sometimes I feel like freedom is near,
C   **Em**
Sometimes I feel like freedom is here,

Sometimes I feel like freedom is so near,
            C7 E7   **F♯m7♭5**
But we're so   far from home.
A7 C7   E7   **F♯m7♭5**
   So   far from home,
                    C7 E7   **F♯m7♭5**
True believer, so   far from home,
            C7 E7   **F♯m7♭5**
But we're so   far from home.

Speed Our Republic

Words and Music by Matthias Keller

Verse 1

F   C F   Bb C7   F
Speed our republic, O Fa - ther on high,
C   C7 F/A C   C7   F G7   C
Lead us in   pathways of justice and right.
C7 F D Gm C7   F   Dm Gm7 C
Rul - ers as well as the ruled, one and   all,
F   D7 Gm   F/C C   F
Girdle with virtue, the ar - mor of might!
F/A Bb   F#°7 Gm D7 Gm F/C   C7   F
Hail! three times hail____ to our coun - try and flag!
C C7 F/A C7/G C7/E   F   Dm Gm7 C
Rulers as   well as   the ruled, one and   all,
F   D7 Gm   F/C C   F
Girdle with virtue, the ar - mor of might!
F/A Bb   F#°7 Gm D7 Gm F/C   C7   F
Hail! three times hail____ to our coun - try and flag!

Verse 2

F   C F   Bb C7   F
Foremost in battle, for freedom to stand,
C C7 F/A C   C7   F   G7   C
We rush to arms when aroused by its call.
C7 F D Gm C7   F   Dm   Gm7 C
Still as of yore when George Washington   led,
F   D7 Gm   F/C C
Thunders our war-cry, we conquer or fall!
F/A Bb   F#°7 Gm D7 Gm F/C   C7   F
Hail! three times hail____ to our coun - try and flag!
C   C7 F/A C7/G C7/E F   Dm   Gm7 C
Still as of yore when George Washington led,
F   D7 Gm   F/C C   F
Thunders our war-cry, we conquer or fall!
F/A Bb   F#°7 Gm D7 Gm F/C   C7   F
Hail! three times hail____ to our coun - try and flag!

Copyright © 2008 Amsco Publications, a Division of Music Sales Corporation.
All Rights Reserved. International Copyright Secured.

Verse 3

F   C   F   B♭ C7 F

Rise up, proud eagle, rise up to the clouds,

C   C7 F/A C C7   F   G7   C

Spread thy broad   wing o'er this fair western world!

C7   F   D Gm C7 F   Dm   Gm7 C

Fling from thy beak our dear banner of   old!

F   D7 Gm   F/C C   F

Show that it   still is for freedom unfurled!

F/A B♭   F♯°7 Gm D7 Gm F/C   C7   F

Hail! three times hail_____ to our coun - try and flag!

C   C7 F/A C7/G C7/E F   Dm   Gm7 C

Fling from thy beak our   dear banner of   old!

F   D7 Gm   F/C C   F

Show that it   still is for freedom unfurled!

F/A B♭   F♯°7 Gm D7 Gm F/C   C7   F

Hail! three times hail_____ to our coun - try and flag!

Springfield Mountain

Traditional

Verse 1

                   G   **D7**
On Springfield Mountain there did dwell
                   G
A comely youth I knew full well.

Chorus

                D7
Too roo de noo, too roo de nay.
                G
Too roo de noo, too roo de nay.

Verse 2

                 D7
One Monday morning he did go,
               G
Down in the meadow for to mow.

Chorus

Verse 3

G   **D7**
He had not mowed quite 'round the field,
               G
When a poison serpent bit his heel.

Chorus

Verse 4

G   **D7**
He took his scythe and with a blow,
              G
He laid the poison serpent low.

Chorus

Verse 5

G   **D7**
He took the serpent in his hand,
                  G
And straight away went to Molly Bland.

Copyright © 2008 Amsco Publications, a Division of Music Sales Corporation.
All Rights Reserved. International Copyright Secured.

Chorus

	G		D7

Verse 6   Now Molly had a ruby lip,

                                   G

    With which the poison she did sip.

Chorus

    G   D7

Verse 7   But Molly had a rotten tooth,

                                   G

    And so the poison killed them both.

Chorus

    G   D7

Verse 8   And all their friends both far and near,

                                   G

    Did howl and cry, they were so dear.

Chorus

    G   D7

Verse 9   Now all you maids, a warning take,

                                   G

    From Molly Bland and Tommy Blake.

                                D7

Chorus   Too roo de noo, too roo de nay.

                                   G

    Too roo de noo, too roo de nay.

The Stars And Stripes Forever

Words and Music by John Philip Sousa

G
Hurrah for the flag of the free.
                               D7
May it wave as our standard forever,

The gem of the land and the sea,
G   **D7**
The banner of the right.
G
Let despots remember the day,
       B   **Em**
When our fathers with might endeavor,
E♭   **G**
Proclaimed as they marched to the fray,

That by their might and by their right,
          D7 G
It waves forev - er.

Copyright © 2008 Amsco Publications, a Division of Music Sales Corporation.
All Rights Reserved. International Copyright Secured.

Sweet Adeline

Words by Richard H. Gerard
Music by Henry W. Armstrong

G7 C
Sweet Adeline,
E7 F   A7/E D7
My Adeline,_____
           G7
At night, dear heart,
D7 D♯°7 C/E
For you I   pine.
G7   C
In all my dreams,
    E7   F   A7/E Dm
Your fair face beams._____
F♯°7   C   A   D7
You're the flower of my heart,
      G7   C
Sweet Adel - ine.

Copyright © 2008 Amsco Publications, a Division of Music Sales Corporation.
All Rights Reserved. International Copyright Secured.

The Star-Spangled Banner

Words by Francis Scott Key
Music by John Stafford Smith

Verse 1

B♭   F/A Gm D7   Gm   C7 F
Oh, say, can you see, by the dawn's early   light,
B♭   F/C B♭/D F   F7   B♭
What so proudly   we   hailed at the twilight's last gleaming,
             F/A Gm D7   Gm C7 F
Whose broad stripes and bright stars, thro' the perilous fight,
B♭ F/C B♭/D F   F7   B♭
O'er the ramparts we   watch'd, were so gallantly streaming?
                         F   F7
And the rockets' red glare, the bombs bursting in air,
B♭   F   F7/E♭ B♭/D Gm C7 F
Gave proof thro' the night that our flag was still there.

Refrain 1

B♭   E♭   G7/D Cm G/D Cm B♭/F F
O say, does that star-spangled ban - ner yet wave,_
F7/E♭ B♭   C7/G B♭/F F7   B♭
O'er the   land of the free and the home of the brave.

Verse 2

B♭   F/A Gm D7   Gm   C7 F
On the shore dimly   seen thro' the mists of the deep,
B♭ F/C B♭/D F   F7   B♭
Where the foe's haughty   host in dread silence reposes,
           F/A Gm   D7   Gm C7 F
What is that which the   breeze, o'er the towering steep,
B♭ F/C B♭/D F   F7   B♭
As it fit - ful - ly   blows, half conceals, half discloses,
                       F   F7
Now it catches the gleam of the morning's first beam,
B♭   F F7/E♭   B♭/D Gm C7 F
In full glory reflected,   now shines on the stream:

Refrain 2

B♭   E♭   G7/D Cm G/D Cm B♭/F F
'Tis the star-spangled banner! O,   long may it   wave__
F7/E♭ B♭   C7/G B♭/F F7   B♭
O'er the   land of the free and the home of the brave!

Copyright © 2008 Amsco Publications, a Division of Music Sales Corporation.
All Rights Reserved. International Copyright Secured.

Verse 3

    B♭   **F/A Gm D7**   **Gm**   **C7 F**
And where is that band who so vauntingly swore,
    B♭ F/C B♭/D F   F7   **B♭**
That the havoc of   war and the battle's confusion,
       F/A Gm D7   **Gm**   **C7 F**
A home and a   country should leave us no more,
    B♭   **F/C B♭/D F   F7**   **B♭**
Their blood has   wash'd out their foul footsteps' pollution.
            F   **F7**
No refuge could save the hireling and slave,
      B♭   **F**   **F7/E♭** **B♭/D Gm C7** **F**
From the terror of flight or the   gloom of the grave:

Refrain 3

     B♭   **E♭**   **G7/D Cm G/D Cm B♭/F F**
And the star-spangled banner in   tri - umph doth wave,___
  F7/E♭ B♭   **C7/G B♭/F F7**   **B♭**
O'er the   land of the free and the home of the brave.

Verse 4

    B♭   **F/A Gm D7**   **Gm**   **C7 F**
O, thus be it   ever when freemen shall stand,
   B♭   **F/C B♭/D F**   **F7**   **B♭**
Between their lov'd home and wild war's desolation;
           F/A Gm D7   **Gm**   **C7**   **F**
Blest with vict'ry and peace, may the heav'n-rescued land,
     B♭   **F/C B♭/D F**   **F7**   **B♭**
Praise the Pow'r that hath   made and preserv'd us as a nation!
                F   **F7**
Then conquer we must, when our cause it is just,
      B♭   **F**   **F7/E♭** **B♭/D Gm C7** **F**
And this be our motto: "In   God is   our trust."

Refrain 4

     B♭   **E♭**   **G7/D Cm G/D Cm** **B♭/F F**
And the star-spangled banner in   tri - umph shall wave,___
  F7/E♭ B♭   **C7/G B♭/F F7**   **B♭**
O'er the   land of the free and the home of the brave.

Steal Away

Traditional

Refrain

F
Steal away, steal away,
B♭ C F
Steal away to Je - sus:

Steal away, steal away home
Dm   F   C   F
I ain't got long to stay here.

Verse 1

B♭   F
My Lord calls me,

He calls me by the thunder;

The trumpet sounds within my soul,
Dm   F   C   F
I ain't got long to stay here.

Refrain

F
Steal away, steal away,
B♭ C F
Steal away to Je - sus:

Steal away, steal away home
Dm   F   C   F
I ain't got long to stay here.

Verse 2

B♭   F
Green trees are bending,

Poor sinners stand trembling,

The trumpet sounds within my soul,
Dm   F   C   F
I ain't got long to stay here.

Copyright © 2008 Amsco Publications, a Division of Music Sales Corporation.
All Rights Reserved. International Copyright Secured.

Refrain

F
Steal away, steal away,
　　　 B♭ C　F
Steal away to Je - sus:

Steal away, steal away home
Dm　　F　　 C　F
I ain't got long to stay here.

Verse 3

B♭　　　　　 F
My Lord calls me,

He calls me by the lightning;

The trumpet sounds within my soul,
Dm　　F　　 C　F
I ain't got long to stay here.

Refrain

F
Steal away, steal away,
　　　 B♭ C　F
Steal away to Je - sus:

Steal away, steal away home
Dm　　F　　 C　F
I ain't got long to stay here.

The Streets Of Laredo

Traditional

Verse 1

D   A7   D   Bm A7
As I was a-walkin' the streets of La– –redo,
D/F♯   G   D   A7
As I walked out in Laredo one day,
D   A7   Bm   A7
I spied a young cowboy all wrapped in white linen,
D/F♯   G   A7   D
All wrapped in white linen as cold as the clay.

Verse 2

         A7   Bm   A7
"I see by your outfit that you are a cowboy"
D/F♯   G   D   A7
These words he did say as I boldly stepped by.
D   A7   Bm   A7
"Come sit down beside me and hear my sad story,
D/F♯   G   A7   D
I was shot in the breast and I know I must die."

Verse 3

         A7   Bm   A7
"It was once in the saddle I used to go dashing,
D/F♯   G   D   A7
Once in the saddle I used to go gay,
D   A7   Bm   A7
First down to Rosie's and then to the card house,
D/F♯   G   A7   D
Got shot in the breast, I am dying today."

Copyright © 2008 Amsco Publications, a Division of Music Sales Corporation.
All Rights Reserved. International Copyright Secured.

Verse 4

A7   Bm   A7
"Get sixteen gamblers to carry my coffin,
D/F♯ G   A7   D
Let six jolly cowboys come sing me a song.
             A7   Bm   A7
Take me to the graveyard and lay the sod o'er me,
D/F♯ G   D   A7
For I'm a poor cowboy and I know I've done wrong."

Verse 5

             A7   Bm   A7
"Oh, bang the drum slowly and play the fife lowly,
D/F♯   G   A7   D
Play the dead march as you carry me along,
            A7   Bm   A7
Put bunches of roses all over my coffin,
D/F♯ G   D   A7
Roses to deaden the clods as they fall."

Sweet Hour Of Prayer

Words by William W. Walford
Music by William B. Bradbury

Verse 1

        C   F
Sweet hour of prayer, sweet hour of prayer,
        C   G
That calls me from a world of care,
        C
And bids me at my Father's throne,
        C   C/G G7 C
Make all my wants and wish - es known.
     G7 C F C
In seasons of distress and grief,
          G7 C   F C   G
My soul has oft - en found relief,
        C   F
And oft escaped the tempter's snare,
     C   C/G G7 C
By thy return, sweet hour of prayer.

Verse 2

        C   F
Sweet hour of prayer, sweet hour of prayer,
        C   G
The joys I feel, the bliss I share,
        C
Of those whose anxious spirits burn,
        C   C/G   G7   C
With strong desires for thy return,
     G7 C F C
With such I hasten to the place,
        G7 C   F C   G
Where God my Savior shows His face,
        C   F
And gladly take my station there,
     C   C/G G7 C
And wait for thee, sweet hour of prayer.

Copyright © 2008 Amsco Publications, a Division of Music Sales Corporation.
All Rights Reserved. International Copyright Secured.

Verse 3

       C   **F**
Sweet hour of prayer, sweet hour of prayer,
    C   **G**
Thy wings shall my petition bear,
    C
To Him whose truth and faithfulness,
    C   **C/G**   **G7 C**
Engage the waiting soul to   bless.
    G7 C F   C
And since He bids me seek His face,
    G7 C F   C G
Believe His Word and trust His grace,
    C   **F**
I'll cast on Him my every care,
      C   **C/G G7 C**
And wait for thee, sweet hour of prayer.

Verse 4

       C   **F**
Sweet hour of prayer, sweet hour of prayer,
    C   **G**
May I thy consolation share,
    C
Till, from Mount Pisgah's lofty height,
 C   **C/G**   **G7 C**
I view my home and take my flight.
    G7 C F   C
This robe of flesh I'll drop and rise,
    G7 C F   C G
To seize the ev - er - lasting prize;
    C   **F**
And shout, while passing through the air,
    C   **C/G G7 C**
"Farewell, farewell, sweet hour of prayer."

Swing Low, Sweet Chariot

Traditional

Chorus

D   Bm   Em7 A7
Swing low, sweet chari–ot,
Bm   F♯m   Em7 A7
Coming for to carry me home,
D   Bm   Gmaj7 Em7 A7
Swing low, sweet chari– – –ot,
D   G   Em7 A7 D
Coming for to carry me home.

Verse 1

                    Gmaj7   A7
I looked over Jordan and what did I see,
Bm   F♯m   Em
Coming for to carry me home?
A7 D   Bm Em7   A7
   A band of angels coming after me,
D   Em7 A7 D
Coming for to carry me home.

Chorus

Verse 2

                    Gmaj7 A7
If you get there before I   do,
Bm   F♯m   Em
Coming for to carry me home,
A7   D   Bm   Em7   A7
   Tell all my friends I'm coming too,
D   Em7 A7 D
Coming for to carry me home.

Chorus

Copyright © 2008 Amsco Publications, a Division of Music Sales Corporation.
All Rights Reserved. International Copyright Secured.

                    Gmaj7 A7
The brightest day that ever I   saw,
Bm   **F♯m**   **Em**
Coming for to carry me home,
A7   **D**   **Bm**   **Em7** **A7**
   When Jesus washed my sins   away,
D   **Em7 A7 D**
Coming for to carry me home.

Chorus

                    Gmaj7   **A7**
Verse 4   I'm sometimes up and sometimes down,
Bm   **F♯m**   **Em**
Coming for to carry me home,
A7   **D**   **Bm**   **Em7**   **A7**
   But still my soul feels heavenly bound,
D   **Em7 A7 D**
Coming for to carry me home.

Chorus

D   **Bm**   **Em7 A7**
Swing low, sweet chari–ot,
Bm   **F♯m**   **Em7 A7**
Coming for to carry me home,
D   **Bm**   **Gmaj7 Em7 A7**
Swing low, sweet chari– – –ot,
D   **G**   **Em7 A7 D**
Coming for to carry me home.

Take Me Out To The Ball Game

Words by Jack Norworth
Music by Albert Von Tilzer

Intro | **Em7** | **B♭7** |

       | **D**   **G** | **D** **D°** **D** |

       | **E7** | **A7** |

       | **D** | |

          A
Take me out to the ball game,
D   **A7**
Take me out to the crowd,
B7   **Em**
Buy me some peanuts and Cracker Jack,
E   **A7**
I don't care if I ever get back.
    D   **A**
Let me root, root, root for the home team,
  D **D7** **G**
If they don't win, it's a shame,
    Em7 B♭ **D**   **G** **D**
For it's one, two, three strikes, you're out,
D° D **E7 A7 D**
At the old ball game.

Copyright © 2008 Amsco Publications, a Division of Music Sales Corporation.
All Rights Reserved. International Copyright Secured.

Tell Me Why

Traditional

Verse 1

G C#° D7 G B7   C   G
Tell___ me why__ the stars do shine,
 C#° D7 G G7 A7 D   D7
Tell   me why the ivy twines,__
G C#° D7 G B7   C   C6 B7
Tell___ me why__ the skies are blue,
E7   A7   D7 G D7 G
And I will tell you why I____ love you.

Verse 2

G C#° D7 G B7   C   G
God___ has made__ the stars to shine,
 C#° D7 G   G7 A7 D   D7
God___ has made the ivy twine,__
G C#° D7 G B7   C   C6 B7
God___ has made__ the skies so blue,
E7   A7   D7 G   D7   G
And God has made you__ that's why I love you.

Copyright © 2008 Amsco Publications, a Division of Music Sales Corporation.
All Rights Reserved. International Copyright Secured.

Sweet And Low

Words by Alfred, Lord Tennyson
Music by Joseph Barnby

Verse 1

```
C          F    G       C
Sweet and low, sweet and low,
Am         D7        Dm7 G
Wind of the western sea,_____
Em  F   C            F
Low, low, breathe and blow,
D7          Am      D7 G
Wind of the western sea,___
            G7      C  C°7 C
Over the rolling waters go,
G                   Am7 D7 G
Come from the dying moon, and blow,
Am         D7    Dm7 Fm
Blow him again to me,_____
C          G
While my little one,
E♭6        G7         C
While my pretty one, sleeps.
```

Verse 2

```
C          F    G       C
Sleep and rest, sleep and rest,
Am         D7      Dm7 G
Father will come to thee   soon;
Em  F   C            F
Rest, rest, on mother's breast,
D7          Am      D7 G
Father will come to thee soon;
            G7    C  C°7 C
Father will come to  his    babe in the nest,
G                   Am7 D7 G
Silver sails all out of the west,
Am         D7    Dm7 Fm
Under the silver moon,___
C          G
Sleep my little one,
E♭6        G7         C
Sleep my pretty one, sleep.
```

Copyright © 2008 Amsco Publications, a Division of Music Sales Corporation.
All Rights Reserved. International Copyright Secured.

Tenting Tonight

Words and Music by William Kittridge

Verse 1

      A   D   A
We're tenting tonight on the old camp-ground,
A/E   E7   A
Give us a song to cheer,
                D   A
Our weary hearts, a song of home,
   E7   D/A E7 A
And friends we love so   dear.

Refrain

                      D
Many are the hearts that are weary tonight,
A   E   A   E
Wishing for the war to end,
A   E   A   D
Many are the hearts looking for the right,
   A/E   E7   A
To see the dawn of peace.
             D
Tenting tonight, tenting tonight,
E7   D/E E7   A
Tenting on the old camp-ground.

Verse 2

          A   D   A
We've been tenting tonight on the old camp-ground,
A/E   E7   A
Thinking of days gone by,
                   D   A
Of the loved ones at home that gave us the hand,
       E7   D/A E7   A
And the tear that said, "Good-bye."

Copyright © 2008 Amsco Publications, a Division of Music Sales Corporation.
All Rights Reserved. International Copyright Secured.

Refrain

                                D
Many are the hearts that are weary tonight,
A   **E**   **A**   **E**
Wishing for the war to end,
A   **E**   **A**   **D**
Many are the hearts looking for the right,
   A/E   **E7**   **A**
To see the dawn of peace.
                   D
Tenting tonight, tenting tonight,
E7   **D/E E7** **A**
Tenting on the old camp-ground.

               A   **D A**
Verse 3
We are tired of war on the old camp-ground,
A/E   **E7**   **A**
Many are the dead and gone,
                    D   **A**
Of the brave and true who've left their homes;
E7   **D/A** **E7 A**
Others been wounded long.

                                  D

Refrain
Many are the hearts that are weary tonight,
A   **E**   **A**   **E**
Wishing for the war to end,
A   **E**   **A**   **D**
Many are the hearts looking for the right,
   A/E   **E7**   **A**
To see the dawn of peace.
                   D
Tenting tonight, tenting tonight,
E7   **D/E E7** **A**
Tenting on the old camp-ground.

        A   **D** **A**
We've been fighting today on the old camp-ground,
A/E   **E7**   **A**
Many are lying near,
                 D   **A**
Some are dead, and some are dying,
E7   **D/A** **E7** **A**
Many are   in   tears.

                       D
Many are the hearts that are weary tonight,
A   **E**   **A**   **E**
Wishing for the war to end,
A   **E**   **A**   **D**
Many are the hearts looking for the light,
   A/E   **E7**   **A**
To see the dawn of peace.
                 D
Dying tonight, tenting tonight,
E7   **D/E** **E7**   **A**
Dying on the old camp-ground.

There Are Many Flags
In Many Lands

Words and Music by Mary H. Howliston

Verse 1

    A E7   D A
There are many flags in many lands,
       E7 A E
There are flags of ev - ery hue.
A   **E7 A D A**
But there is no flag however grand,
     D Bm E7   **A**
Like our own Red, White and Blue.

Refrain

E   **A**
Then hurrah for the flag, our country's flag.
    D **F♯7 Bm C♯m7 E**
Its stripes and white stars, too.
A   **E7 A D A**
There is no flag in any land,
     D Bm E7   **A**
Like our own Red, White and Blue.

Verse 2

    A E7   **D A**
I know where the prettiest colors are,
      E7 A E
And I'm sure if I on - ly knew,
A   **E7 A D**   **A**
How to get them here I'd make a flag,
    D **Bm E7**   **A**
Of glorious Red, White and Blue.

Refrain

E   **A**
Then hurrah for the flag, our country's flag.
    D **F♯7 Bm C♯m7 E**
Its stripes and white stars, too.
A   **E7 A D A**
There is no flag in any land,
     D Bm E7   **A**
Like our own Red, White and Blue.

Copyright © 2008 Amsco Publications, a Division of Music Sales Corporation.
All Rights Reserved. International Copyright Secured.

Verse 3

A   E7   D   A
I would cut a piece from the evening sky,
             E7 A E
Where the stars are shining through,
A   E7 A D A
And use it, just as it sits on high,
        D Bm E7   A
For my stars and field of blue.

Refrain

E   A
Then hurrah for the flag, our country's flag.
      D   F♯7 Bm C♯m7 E
Its stripes and white stars,   too.
A   E7 A D A
There is no flag in any land,
        D Bm E7   A
Like our own Red, White and Blue.

Verse 4

         A   E7   D A
Then I'd want a piece of fleecy cloud,
              E7 A E
And then some red from a rainbow bright;
A   E7 A D A
And put them together, side by side,
        D   Bm E7   A
For my stripes of   red and white.

Refrain

E   A
Then hurrah for the flag, our country's flag.
      D   F♯7 Bm C♯m7 E
Its stripes and white stars,   too.
A   E7 A D A
There is no flag in any land,
        D Bm E7   A
Like our own Red, White and Blue.

Verse 5

           A   **E7**   **D**   **A**
We shall always love the stars and stripes,
           E7 A E
And we ever shall be true.
A   **E7 A D A**
To this land of ours and the dear old flag,
         D   **Bm** **E7 A**
Our own Red, White and Blue.

Refrain

          E   **A**
Then hurrah for the flag, our country's flag.
     D   **F♯7 Bm** **C♯m7 E**
Its stripes and white stars,   too.
A   **E7 A D A**
There is no flag in any land,
       D   **Bm** **E7**   **A**
Like our own Red, White and Blue.

Turkey In The Straw

Traditional

Verse 1

    F
As I was going down the road,
          G   **C7**
With a tired team and a heavy load,
   F
I cracked my whip and the leader sprung,
   F/A **B♭**   **F** **C7** **F**
From day to day on the wagon tongue.

Refrain

F
Turkey in the hay, turkey in the straw,
B♭
Turkey in the hay, turkey in the straw,
F   **C**
Roll 'em up, twist 'em up, high tuck-a-haw,
C7 **F**   **C7** **F**
And hit 'em up a tune called "Turkey in the Straw."

Verse 2

    F
Oh, I went out to milk, and I didn't know how,
         G   **C7**
I milked the goat instead of the cow,
   F
A monkey sittin' on a pile of straw,
  F/A   **B♭**   **F**   **C7** **F**
A-winkin' at his mother-in - law.

Refrain

F
Turkey in the hay, turkey in the straw,
B♭
Turkey in the hay, turkey in the straw,
F   **C**
Roll 'em up, twist 'em up, high tuck-a-haw,
C7 **F**   **C7** **F**
And hit 'em up a tune called "Turkey in the Straw."

Copyright © 2008 Amsco Publications, a Division of Music Sales Corporation.
All Rights Reserved. International Copyright Secured.

Verse 3

    F
Well, I met Mr. Catfish comin' downstream,
      G   **C7**
Says Mr. Catfish, "What does you mean?"
F
Caught Mr. Catfish by the snout,
  F/A   **B♭** **F** **C7** **F**
And turned that catfish wrong side out.

Refrain

F
Turkey in the hay, turkey in the straw,
B♭
Turkey in the hay, turkey in the straw,
F   **C**
Roll 'em up, twist 'em up, high tuck-a-haw,
C7 **F**   **C7** **F**
And hit 'em up a tune called "Turkey in the Straw."

Verse 4

     F
Then I came to a river and I couldn't get across,
       G   **C7**
So, I paid five dollars for a old blind horse,
F
Well, he wouldn't go ahead, and he wouldn't stand still,
  F/A   **B♭**   **F** **C7** **F**
So he went up and down like an old saw mill.

Refrain

F
Turkey in the hay, turkey in the straw,
B♭
Turkey in the hay, turkey in the straw,
F   **C**
Roll 'em up, twist 'em up, high tuck-a-haw,
C7 **F**   **C7** **F**
And hit 'em up a tune called "Turkey in the Straw."

Verse 5

      F
As I came down the new cut road,
                 G   **C7**
I met Mr. Bullfrog, I met Miss Toad,
      F
And every time Miss Toad would sing,
     F/A   **B♭** **F** **C7** **F**
Ole bullfrog cut a pi - geon wing.

Refrain

      F
Turkey in the hay, turkey in the straw,
B♭
Turkey in the hay, turkey in the straw,
F   **C**
Roll 'em up, twist 'em up, high tuck-a-haw,
C7 **F**   **C7**   **F**
And hit 'em up a tune called "Turkey in the Straw."

Verse 6

       F
Oh, I jumped in the seat, and I gave a little yell,
                      G   **C7**
The horses ran away, broke the wagon all to hell.
F
Sugar in the gourd and honey in the horn,
   F/A   **B♭**   **F** **C7** **F**
I never been so happy since the hour I was born.

Refrain

      F
Turkey in the hay, turkey in the straw,
B♭
Turkey in the hay, turkey in the straw,
F   **C**
Roll 'em up, twist 'em up, high tuck-a-haw,
C7 **F**   **C7** **F**
And hit 'em up a tune called "Turkey in the Straw."

Wabash Cannonball

Traditional

Verse 1

          G
From the great Atlantic Ocean,
G7 **C**
To the wide Pacific shore,
Am   **D7**   **D**
From the ones we leave behind us,
      G   **C**   **G**
To the ones we see once more.

She's mighty tall and handsome,
G7 **C**
And quite well known by all,
D7
How we love the choo-choo,
         G
Of the Wabash Cannonball.

Chorus

         G
Hear the bell and whistle calling,
G7   **C**
Hear the wheels that go "clack-clack,"
G7   **D**
Hear the roaring of the engine,
     G **C**   **G**
As she rolls along the track.

The magic of the railroad,
G7 **C**
Wins hearts of one and all,
   D7
As we reach our destination,
         G
On the Wabash Cannonball.

Copyright © 2008 Amsco Publications, a Division of Music Sales Corporation.
All Rights Reserved. International Copyright Secured.

Verse 2

        G
Listen to the rhythmic jingle,
G7   **C**
And the rumble and the roar,
Am **D7**   **D**
As she glides along the woodlands,
             G   **C** **G**
Through the hills and by the shore.

You hear the mighty engine,
G7 **C**
And pray that it won't stall,
D7
While we safely travel
             G
On the Wabash Cannonball.

Chorus

Verse 3

          G
She was coming from Atlanta,
G7 **C**
On a cold December day.
Am **D7**   **D**
As she rolled into the station,
        G   **C**   **G**
I could hear a woman say,

"He's mighty big and handsome,
G7 **C**
And sure did make me fall,
D7
He's a-comin' toward me
            G
On the Wabash Cannonball."

Chorus

253

We Plough The Fields And Scatter

Words by Matthias Claudius
Music by Johann Abraham Peter Schülz

Verse 1

   A   E   A
We plough the fields and scatter,
  D   B7 E
The good seed on the land,
A E B7 E A E B7 C♯m
But it is fed and wat - ered,
   A   B7   E
By God's almighty hand:
        A   E7
He sends the snow in winter,
  A   E7   E
The warmth to swell the grain,
  A   E   F♯m
The breezes and the sunshine,
 Bm E7   A
And soft, refreshing rain.

Refrain

        E
All good gifts around us,
   A   E7 A E
Are sent from heav'n a - bove.
    A   E A E F♯m C♯ F♯m
Then thank the Lord, O thank the Lord,
A D A E A
For all__ his love.

Copyright © 2008 Amsco Publications, a Division of Music Sales Corporation.
All Rights Reserved. International Copyright Secured.

Verse 2

     A   **E** **A**
He only is the maker,
  D   **B7**   **E**
Of all things near and far,
A **E**   **B7 E** **A** **E** **B7** **C♯m**
He paints the wayside flow - er,
  A   **B7**   **E**
He lights the evening star;
            A   **E7**
The winds and waves obey him,
  A   **E7**   **E**
By him the birds are fed;
    A   **E**   **F♯m**
Much more to us, his children,
  Bm   **E7** **A**
He gives our daily bread.

Refrain

             E
All good gifts around us,
    A   **E7**   **A E**
Are sent from heav'n a - bove.
    A   **E A**   **E F♯m** **C♯** **F♯m**
Then thank the Lord, O thank the Lord,
A **D A E** **A**
For all__ his love.

    A   **E A**
We thank thee then, O Father,
    D   **B7**   **E**
For all things bright and good,
A E   B7 E A E B7 C♯m
The seed time and the har - vest,
    A   **B7**   **E**
Our life, our health, our food.
         A   **E7**
Accept the gifts we offer,
    A   **E7**   **E**
For all thy love imparts,
    A   **E**   **F♯m**
And what thou most desirest,
   Bm   **E7**   **A**
Our humble, thankful hearts.

           E
All good gifts around us,
    A   **E7**   **A E**
Are sent from heav'n a - bove.
      A   **E A**   **E F♯m C♯ F♯m**
Then thank the Lord, O thank the Lord,
A D A E A
For all__ his love.

You're A Grand Old Flag

Words and Music by George M. Cohan

Intro

G		
D7		
A7	C Cm D7
G	

Chorus

D7   G   C G
You're a grand old flag,
D7   G
You're a high flying flag,
D7   G   D7 G
And forev - er in peace,
G♯°   D7
May you wave.

You're the emblem of,
   G
The land I love.
   A7   D7   Am F7 D7
The home of the free and the brave._____
     G
Ev'ry heart beats true,
D7   G
'Neath the Red, White and Blue,
Bm   Dm   E7   Am
Where there's never a boast or brag.
D7   G   D7
But should auld acquaintance be forgot,
       A7   C   Cm G
Keep your eye on the grand old flag.

Copyright © 2008 Amsco Publications, a Division of Music Sales Corporation.
All Rights Reserved. International Copyright Secured.

When Johnny Comes Marching Home

Words and Music by Patrick S. Gilmore

Verse 1

Em
When Johnny comes marching home again,
G
Hurrah! Hurrah!
Em
We'll give him a hearty welcome then,
G   **B7**
Hurrah! Hurrah!

The men will cheer and the boys will shout.
Cmaj7   **B7**
The ladies they will all turn out.
Em Am Em
And we'll all   feel gay,
B   Em   **D Em**
When Johnny comes marching home.

Verse 2

Em
Get ready for the Jubilee,
G
Hurrah! Hurrah!
Em
We'll give the hero three times three,
G   **B7**
Hurrah! Hurrah!

The laurel wreath is ready now,
Cmaj7   **B7**
To place upon his loyal brow.
Em Am Em
And we'll all   feel gay,
B   Em   **D Em**
When Johnny comes marching home.

Copyright © 2008 Amsco Publications, a Division of Music Sales Corporation.
All Rights Reserved. International Copyright Secured.

Verse 3

Em
The old church bell will peal with joy,
G
Hurrah! Hurrah!
Em
To welcome home our darling boy,
G　　**B7**
Hurrah! Hurrah!

The village lads and lassies say,
　　Cmaj7　　　**B7**
With roses they will strew the way.
　　　Em Am Em
And we'll all　　feel　gay,
B　　**Em**　　　　　**D Em**
When Johnny comes marching home.

Verse 4

Em
Let love and friendship on that day,
G
Hurrah! Hurrah!
Em
Their choicest treasures then display,
G　　**B7**
Hurrah! Hurrah!

And let each one perform some part,
　　Cmaj7　　　**B7**
To fill with joy the warrior's heart.
　　　Em Am Em
And we'll all　　feel　gay,
B　　**Em**　　　　　**D Em**
When Johnny comes marching home.

We Wish You A Merry Christmas

Traditional

Verse 1

    G   **C**
We wish you a merry Christmas,
E   A7   **D7**
We wish you a merry Christmas,
    G   **C**
We wish you a merry Christmas,
    Am7 D7 G
And a happy New Year.

Refrain

          D
Good tidings we bring,
    A7   **D**
To all of you here,
    G
Good tidings for Christmas,
    Am7 D7   G
And a happy New Year.
    G   **C**
We wish you a merry Christmas,
E   A7   **D7**
We wish you a merry Christmas,
    G   **C**
We wish you a merry Christmas,
    Am7 D7 G
And a happy New Year.

Verse 2

    G   **C**
Oh, bring us some figgy pudding,
E   A7   **D7**
Oh, bring us some figgy pudding,
    G   **C**
Oh, bring us a figgy pudding,
    Am7 D7 G
And a cup of good cheer.

Copyright © 2008 Amsco Publications, a Division of Music Sales Corporation.
All Rights Reserved. International Copyright Secured.

Refrain

                    D
Good tidings we bring,
       A7   D
To all of you here,
          G
Good tidings for Christmas,
       Am7 D7   G
And a happy New Year.
       G   C
We wish you a merry Christmas,
E A7   D7
We wish you a merry Christmas,
       G   C
We wish you a merry Christmas,
       Am7 D7 G
And a happy New Year.

Verse 3

          G   C
We won't go until we get some,
E   A7   D7
We won't go until we get some,
       G   C
We won't go until we get some,
       Am7 D7 G
So bring it right here.

Refrain

                    D
Good tidings we bring,
       A7   D
To all of you here,
          G
Good tidings for Christmas,
       Am7 D7   G
And a happy New Year.
       G   C
We wish you a merry Christmas,
E   A7   D7
We wish you a merry Christmas,
       G   C
We wish you a merry Christmas,
       Am7 D7 G
And a happy New Year.

Were You There

Traditional

Intro

| B♭ | | F | Dm | |

| Gm7 | C7 | F | B♭ | |

| F | | |

Verse 1

              Dm   **Gm** **C7**   **F**   **B♭ F**
Were you there when they crucified my Lord?_____
              Am   **B♭** **F**   **C**
Were you there when they crucified my Lord?
F B♭ F B♭ F   **Dm**   **B♭**   **F**
Oh,_____ sometimes it causes me to tremble, tremble, tremble.
B♭   **F**   **Dm**   **B♭ C7**   **F**   **B♭ F**
Were you there when they crucified my Lord?_____

Verse 2

              Dm   **Gm** **C7 F**   **B♭** **F**
Were you there when they nailed him to the tree?__
              Am   **B♭** **F**   **C**
Were you there when they nailed him to the tree?
F B♭ F B♭ F   **Dm**   **B♭**   **F**
Oh,_____ sometimes it causes me to tremble, tremble, tremble.
B♭   **F**   **Dm**   **B♭** **C7 F**   **B♭ F**
Were you there when they nailed him to the tree?__

Verse 3

              Dm   **Gm C7 F**   **B♭**   **F**
Were you there when they laid him in the tomb?__
              Am   **B♭ F**   **C**
Were you there when they laid him in the tomb?
F B♭ F B♭ F   **Dm**   **B♭**   **F**
Oh,_____ sometimes it causes me to tremble, tremble, tremble.
B♭   **F**   **Dm**   **B♭ C7** **F**   **B♭**   **F**
Were you there when they laid him in the tomb?__

Copyright © 2008 Amsco Publications, a Division of Music Sales Corporation.
All Rights Reserved. International Copyright Secured.

Verse 4

               Dm   **Gm** **C7** **F**   **B♭** **F**

Were you there when God raised him from the tomb?__

              Am   **B♭**   **F**   **C**

Were you there when God raised him from the tomb?

F **B♭** **F** **B♭** **F**   **Dm**   **B♭**   **F**

Oh,____ sometimes it causes me to tremble, tremble, tremble.

B♭   **F**   **Dm**   **B♭** **C7** **F**   **B♭** **F**

Were you there when God raised him from the tomb?__

What A Friend We Have In Jesus

Words by Joseph Scriven
Music by Charles C. Converse

Verse 1

F   Bb
What a friend we have in Jesus,
F   C7
All our sins and griefs to bear!
F   Bb
What a privilege to carry
F C7   F
Ev'rything to God in prayer!
C7   F
O what peace we often forfeit,
Bb F   C7
O what needless pain we bear,
F   Bb
All because we do not carry
F/C C7   F
Everything to God in prayer!

Verse 2

F   Bb
Have we trials and temptations?
F   C7
Is there trouble anywhere?
F   Bb
We should never be discouraged;
F C7   F
Take it to the Lord in prayer!
C7   F
Can we find a friend so faithful
Bb F   C7
Who will all our sorrows share?
F   Bb
Jesus knows our every weakness;
F/C C7   F
Take it to the Lord in prayer.

Copyright © 2008 Amsco Publications, a Division of Music Sales Corporation.
All Rights Reserved. International Copyright Secured.

Verse 3

F   B♭
Are we weak and heavy laden,
F   C7
Cumbered with a load of care?
F   B♭
Precious Savior, still our refuge;
F   C7   F
Take it to the Lord in prayer!
C7   F
Do thy friends despise, forsake thee?
B♭   F   C7
Take it to the Lord in prayer!
F   B♭
In his arms he'll take and shield thee;
F/C   C7   F
Thou wilt find a solace there.

When I Survey The Wondrous Cross

Words by Isaac Watts
Music by Edward Miller

Verse 1

F B♭ C7   F   B♭   F
When I____ sur - vey the wondrous cross,
       B♭   F C7   F   C
On which the Prince of glo - ry died,___
G7 C   G7 C   C7 F   G7 C
My richest gain I   count but loss,
F   C7 F   Gm   G7 F   C7 F
And pour contempt on   all my pride.

Verse 2

   F   B♭ C7   F   B♭   F
Forbid it,   Lord, that I should boast,
       B♭   F C7   F C
Save in the death of Christ my God!
G7 C   G7 C   C7 F   G7 C
All the vain things that charm me most,
F C7   F   Gm G7   F C7 F
I sac - ri - fice   them to His blood.

Verse 3

   F   B♭ C7   F   B♭   F
See from His head, His hands, His feet,
       B♭   F   C7   F C
Sorrow and love flow mingled down!
G7 C   G7   C   C7   F G7 C
Did e'er such love and sorrow meet,
F   C7   F   Gm G7 F   C7 F
Or thorns compose so rich a   crown?

Verse 4

   F B♭ C7   F   B♭ F
His dying crimson, like a   robe,
       B♭ F   C7 F C
Spreads o'er His body on   the tree,
G7   C G7 C   C7   F G7 C
Then I am dead to   all the globe,
F   C7 F   Gm   G7 F   C7 F
And all   the globe is   dead to   me.

Copyright © 2008 Amsco Publications, a Division of Music Sales Corporation.
All Rights Reserved. International Copyright Secured.

      F B♭   C7 F B♭   F
Were the whole realm of nature mine,
            B♭ F C7 F C
That were a present far   too small,
G7 C G7 C   C7 F G7 C
Love so a - maz - ing, so div - ine,
F   C7 F Gm G7 F   C7 F
Demands my soul, my life, my all.

When The Saints Go Marching In

Traditional

Verse 1
```
       D         D7 G
I'm just a weary    pilgrim,
       D                    A
Plodding through this world of sin.
       D         D7 G
Getting ready for that city,
             D      A7      D
When the saints go marching in.
```

Chorus
```
When the saints go marching in,
                           A
When the saints go marching in,
       D         D7    G
Lord, I want to be in that number,
             D      A7      D
When the saints go marching in.
```

Verse 2
```
       D         D7 G
My father loved the  Savior,
       D             A
What a soldier he had been!
       D         D7    G
But his steps will be more steady,
             D      A7      D
When the saints go marching in.
```

Chorus
```
When the saints go marching in,
                           A
When the saints go marching in,
       D         D7    G
Lord, I want to be in that number,
             D      A7      D
When the saints go marching in.
```

Copyright © 2008 Amsco Publications, a Division of Music Sales Corporation.
All Rights Reserved. International Copyright Secured.

Verse 3

       D   **D7 G**
My mother, may God bless her,
       D   **A**
I can see her now as then.
       D   **D7 G**
With a robe of white a– –round her,
          D   **A7**   **D**
When the saints go marching in.

Chorus

       D   **D7 G**
Verse 4   Up there I'll see the Savior,
       D   **A**
Who redeemed my soul from sin.
       D   **D7 G**
With extended hands He'll greet me,
          D   **A7**   **D**
When the saints go marching in.

Chorus   When the saints go marching in,
                    A
When the saints go marching in,
       D   **D7**   **G**
Lord, I want to be in that number,
       D   **A7**   **D**
When the saints go marching in.

Will The Circle Be Unbroken?

Traditional

Verse 1
        G
I was standing by my window,
   C   **G**
On one cold and cloudy day,

When I saw that hearse come rolling,
  A7   **D7**
For to take my mother away.

Chorus
        G
Will the circle be unbroken,
    C   **G**
By and by, Lord, by and by?
     C   **G**
There's a better home awaiting,
  D **D7**   **G**
In the sky, Lord, in the sky.

Verse 2
        G
Oh, I told the undertaker,
    C   **G**
Undertaker please drive slow,

For this lady you are carrying,
  A7   **D7**
Lord, I hate to see her go.

Chorus

Verse 3
        G
I will follow close behind her,
    C   **G**
Try to hold up and be brave,

But I could not hide my sorrow,
  A7   **D7**
When they laid her in the grave.

Copyright © 2008 Amsco Publications, a Division of Music Sales Corporation.
All Rights Reserved. International Copyright Secured.

Chorus

Verse 4
            G
I went back home, my home was lonesome,
       C   **G**
Missed my mother, she was gone,

All of my brothers, sisters crying,
     A7   **D7**
What a home so sad and lone.

Chorus

Verse 5
           G
We sang the songs of childhood,
       C   **G**
Hymns of faith that made us strong,

Ones that mother Maybelle taught us,
     A7   **D7**
Hear the angels sing along.

Chorus
          G
Will the circle be unbroken,
     C   **G**
By and by, Lord, by and by?
      C   **G**
There's a better home awaiting,
    D **D7**   **G**
In the sky, Lord, in the sky.

Wondrous Love

Words by Alex Means
Traditional

Verse 1

      Dm   **Am**   **Dm**
What wondrous love is this,
C   **Dm**   **Am**
Oh, my soul, oh, my soul,
       F   **Am** **Dm**
What wondrous love is this,
C **Am Dm**
Oh, my   soul,
C   **Dm**   **F**   **Dm**
What wondrous love is this,
              C   **Dm**
That caused the Lord of bliss,
      Am   **Dm** **C**   **Dm**
To bear the dreadful curse for my soul,
      Am
For my soul,
   F   **Am**   **Dm** **C**   **Dm**
To bear the dreadful curse for my soul.

Verse 2

      Dm **Am**   **Dm**
When I was sinking down,
C   **Dm**   **Am**
Sinking down, sinking down,
       F   **Am**   **Dm**
When I was sinking down,
C **Am Dm**
Sinking down,
C   **Dm** **F**   **Dm**
When I was sinking down,
              C   **Dm**
Beneath God's righteous frown,
      Am   **Dm** **C**   **Dm**
Christ laid aside His crown for my soul,
      Am
For my soul,
   F   **Am**   **Dm** **C**   **Dm**
Christ laid aside His crown for my soul.

Copyright © 2008 Amsco Publications, a Division of Music Sales Corporation.
All Rights Reserved. International Copyright Secured.

Verse 3

   Dm **Am** **Dm**
And when from death I'm free,
C **Dm**   **Am**
I'll sing on, I'll sing on,
   F   **Am** **Dm**
And when from death I'm free,
C **Am Dm**
I'll sing on,
C **Dm**   **F**   **Dm**
And when from death I'm free,
    C **Dm**
I'll sing and joyful be,
  Am **Dm C** **Dm**
And through e - ternity,
    Am
I'll sing on, I'll sing on,
    F   **Am Dm C** **Dm**
And through eternity, I'll sing on.

273

Yankee Doodle

Traditional

Verse 1

G   D7
Fath'r and I went down to camp,
G   D7
Along with Captain Gooding,
    G   C
And there we saw the men and boys,
D7   G
As thick as hasty pudding.

Refrain

C
Yankee Doodle, keep it up,
G
Yankee Doodle Dandy,
C
Mind the music and the step,
   G   D7   G
And with the girls be handy.

Verse 2

    G   D7
And there we saw a thousand men,
   G   D7
As rich as Squire David,
    G   C
And what they wasted ev'ry day,
D7   G
I wish it could be sav'd

Refrain

C
Yankee Doodle, keep it up,
G
Yankee Doodle Dandy,
C
Mind the music and the step,
   G   D7   G
And with the girls be handy.

Copyright © 2008 Amsco Publications, a Division of Music Sales Corporation.
All Rights Reserved. International Copyright Secured.

Verse 3

       G   **D7**
And there was Captain Washington,
  G   **D7**
Upon a slapping stallion,
   G   **C**
A-giving orders to his men,
D7   **G**
I guess there was a million.

Refrain

  C
Yankee Doodle, keep it up,
G
Yankee Doodle Dandy,
C
Mind the music and the step,
   G   **D7**   **G**
And with the girls be handy.

Verse 4

     G   **D7**
And then I saw a swamping gun,
    G   **D7**
Large as a log of maple,
  G   **C**
Upon a deuced little cart;
D7   **G**
A load for father's cattle.

Refrain

  C
Yankee Doodle, keep it up,
G
Yankee Doodle Dandy,
C
Mind the music and the step,
   G   **D7**   **G**
And with the girls be handy.

Verse 5

    G   **D7**
And every time they fired it off,
   G   **D7**
It takes a horn of powder,
 G   **C**
It makes a noise like father's gun,
D7   **G**
Only a nation louder.

Refrain

C
Yankee Doodle, keep it up,
G
Yankee Doodle Dandy,
C
Mind the music and the step,
    G   **D7**   **G**
And with the girls be handy.

Verse 6

      G   **D7**
And there I saw a little keg,
  G   **D7**
Its head all made of leather,
     G   **C**
They knocked upon't with little sticks,
D7   **G**
To call the folks together.

Refrain

C
Yankee Doodle, keep it up,
G
Yankee Doodle Dandy,
C
Mind the music and the step,
    G   **D7**   **G**
And with the girls be handy.

Verse 7

      G   **D7**
The troopers then would gallop up,
      G   **D7**
And fire right in our faces;
    G   **C**
It scared me almost half to death,
  D7   **G**
To see them run such races.

Refrain

  C
Yankee Doodle, keep it up,
G
Yankee Doodle Dandy,
C
Mind the music and the step,
    G   **D7**   **G**
And with the girls be handy.

Verse 8

  G   **D7**
Yankee Doodle went to town,
  G   **D7**
A-riding on a pony,
G   **C**
Stuck a feather in his cap,
  D7   **G**
And called it macaroni.

Refrain

  C
Yankee Doodle, keep it up,
G
Yankee Doodle Dandy,
C
Mind the music and the step,
   G   **D7**   **G**
And with the girls be handy.

Yankee Doodle Dandy

Words and Music by George M. Cohan

G   **A7**
I'm a Yankee Doodle Dandy,
D7   **G**
Yankee Doodle, do or die;
E7   **Am E7 Am**
Real live nephew of my Un - cle Sam's,
A7   **D7**
Born on the Fourth of July.
G   **A7**
Got a Yankee Doodle sweetheart,
D7   **G**
She's my Yankee Doodle joy,

Yankee Doodle came to London,

Just to ride the ponies,
A7   **D7**   **G**
I am the Yankee Doodle boy.

Copyright © 2008 Amsco Publications, a Division of Music Sales Corporation.
All Rights Reserved. International Copyright Secured.

The Yellow Rose Of Texas

Traditional

Verse 1

        C
There's a Yellow Rose of Texas,

That I am going to see,
       C#° **Dm**
No other fellow knows her,
D7 **G7**
No - body, only me.
      C
She cried so when I left her,

It like to broke her heart,
   G7   **C**   **F**
And if we ever meet again,
   C   **G7**   **C**
We never more shall part.

Refrain

        C
She's the sweetest rose of color,

A fellow ever knew,
       C#°   **Dm**   **F**
Her eyes are bright as diamonds,_
   D7   **G7**
They sparkle like the dew.
      C
You may talk about your dearest maids,

And sing of Rosy Lee,
   G7   **C**
But the Yellow Rose of Texas,
F   **C**   **G7**   **C**
Beats the belles of Tennessee.

Copyright © 2008 Amsco Publications, a Division of Music Sales Corporation.
All Rights Reserved. International Copyright Secured.

Verse 2

            C

Down beside the Rio Grande,

The stars were shinging bright,
           C#°   **Dm**
We walked along the river,
D7 **G7**
On a quiet summer night,
     C
She said "If you remember,

We parted long ago,
    G7   **C**   **F**
You promised to come back again,
    C   **G7**   **C**
And never leave me so."

Refrain

            C

She's the sweetest rose of color,

A fellow ever knew,
          C#°   **Dm**   **F**
Her eyes are bright as diamonds,_
   D7   **G7**
They sparkle like the dew.
        C
You may talk about your dearest maids,

And sing of Rosy Lee,
    G7   **C**
But the Yellow Rose of Texas,
F   **C**   **G7**   **C**
Beats the belles of Tennessee.

Verse 3

        C
Oh, I'm going back to find her,

My heart is full of woe,
        C♯°   **Dm**
We'll sing the songs together,
D7 **G7**
We sang so long ago,
      C
I'll pick the banjo daily,

And sing the songs of yore,
    G7   **C**   **F**
Then Yellow Rose of Texas,
         C   **G7 C**
She'll be mine forever more.

Refrain

        C
She's the sweetest rose of color,

A fellow ever knew,
       C♯°   **Dm**   **F**
Her eyes are bright as diamonds,_
    D7   **G7**
They sparkle like the dew.
     C
You may talk about your dearest maids,

And sing of Rosy Lee,
   G7   **C**
But the Yellow Rose of Texas,
F   **C**   **G7**   **C**
Beats the belles of Tennessee.

You're In The Army Now

Traditional

Verse 1

        G
You're in the Army now,
           D7
You're not behind a plow,
      G
You'll never get rich,

A-digging a ditch,
         D7   **G**
You're in the Army now.

Verse 2

        G
You're in the Army now,
       D7
You're in the Army now,
      G
You'll never get rich,

On the salary which,
          D7   **G**
You'll get in the Army now.

Copyright © 2008 Amsco Publications, a Division of Music Sales Corporation.
All Rights Reserved. International Copyright Secured.

Chord Finder

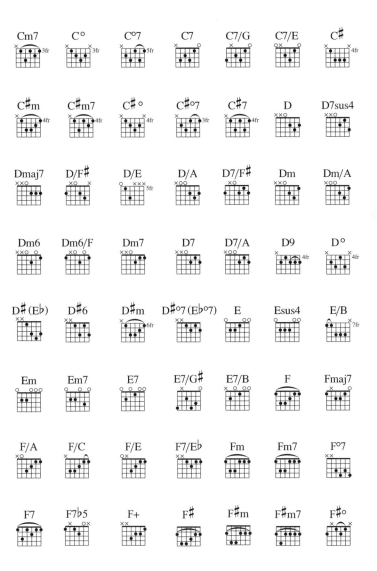